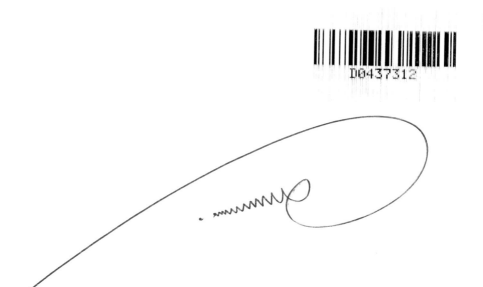

Ze'ev Kolman
250 West 57th Street
Suite 630
New York, NY   10107

The Secret of Healing

The Healing Powers of Ze'ev Kolman

The Secret
of Healing

The Healing Powers
of Ze'ev Kolman

by

Professor Hans Holzer, Ph.D.

Author of *Healing Beyond Medicine: Alternative Paths to Wellness*

BEYOND
WORDS
Publishing
I   N   C

Beyond Words Publishing, Inc.
4443 NE Airport Road
Hillsboro, Oregon 97124-6074
503-693-8700
1-800-284-9673

The information contained in this book is intended to be educational and not for diagnosis, prescription, or treatment of any health disorder whatsoever. This information should not replace competent medical care. The author and publisher are in no way liable for any use or misuse of the material.

Design and typesetting: William H. Brunson Typography Services

Jacket design/calligraphy: Bill McConaughy, Anderson McConaughy Design

Printed in the United States of America
Distributed to the book trade by Publishers Group West

The corporate mission of Beyond Words Publishing, Inc.:
Inspire to Integrity

Library of Congress Cataloging-in-Publication Data
Holzer, Hans.
    The secret of healing : the healing powers of Ze'ev Kolman / by Hans Holzer.
        p.   cm.
    ISBN 1-885223-20-X (cloth)
    1. Kolman, Ze'ev.   2. Mental healing.   3. Mental healing—case studies.   I. Title.
    RZ408.K65H65   1996
    615.8'52—dc20   95-42451
                                                                      CIP

I wish to dedicate my healing work
to the memory of my parents
and to the love of my wife and children.
—Ze'ev Kolman

TABLE OF CONTENTS

PART TWO

PART THREE

Foreword

Ze'ev Kolman, the subject of this book, is a natural healer. His healing—bioenergy—comes from his body energy, which emanates through his hands. His gift—his ability—has nothing to do with one's belief or disbelief or with any form of religious or quasi-religious commitment in order for it to work. It works nearly always, depending on circumstances and the nature, duration, and severity of the disease. Mr. Kolman is not a miracle worker or guru leading some sort of occult movement of faithful followers. He is an ordinary, honest man to whom the gift of healing comes as much as a surprise as it does to those he sees and tries to help.

He is not a medical or other kind of doctor, and he makes no claims whatever to treat the sick the way the medical profession does. But medical doctors frequently work with him, or consult him when all else fails, in order to help the sufferer. That is as it should be: the best of both worlds, the traditional medical approach and the alternative approach, complementing each other.

When Mr. Kolman speaks of patients, he does not pretend to be a doctor and does not treat them the way a conventional physician does, nor does he claim to, either directly or indirectly. But the word *patient* means sufferer, and *treating* means addressing a situation. I am a professional parapsychologist; people seek me out for help with such unusual phenomena as possession, and they are, in that sense, my *patients*. I *treat* their problems, either by discussion and investigation or by hypnotherapy. They know that I am not a medical doctor, even if I am styled Dr. Holzer. The traditional medical profession does not have an exclusive on the terms *patient* or *treatment*.

What Mr. Kolman has to offer is made very clear to all those who seek him out: to be treated through the bioenergetic ability he possesses and has proven to the world at large—and to a number of scientists and medical doctors as well. It is important to know this, for among the many who offer nontraditional healing are a fair number of ineffective practitioners, and a handful of charlatans, too.

But Mr. Kolman is for real, and in these pages you will learn why, how, and what he has done and what he might conceivably do for you, should you require his services. Mr. Kolman, like any genuine bioenergetic healer, cannot guarantee anything but his best effort.

Professor Hans Holzer, Ph.D.

Introduction

It is inevitable that an individual who can bring good health to sufferers is a much sought after person. In ancient and medieval times, that person was in some fashion connected with the world of religion, mainstream or otherwise. Few were the true medical doctors who stood above the rest of the profession because of their skills and knowledge. But a mystic, a guru, a healer beyond the boundaries of science would gather much more attention and, because of using an unconventional approach, touch the emotions of those seeking help.

As we approach the twenty-first century, the Age of Reason has become a bit shoddy around the edges. Science, especially empiric science, alone no longer has all the answers, and more and more questions remain without response by the very people whose training should have prepared them to deliver such response.

Gradually, the notion of our spiritual nature is becoming a respectable topic and a reality to those not bound to outmoded traditions in their quests for health. Even religion, in all its shades and versions, cannot ignore the fact that, if humanity was created in God's image, why then are humans not also in perfect health?

People like Edgar Cayce have long pointed out that humans are indeed meant to be in perfect health, and when they are not, the entire person needs to be dealt with, not just the body alone. Modern medicine addresses the symptoms rather than the causes, concentrating on giving immediate relief to those who are in pain— a commendable notion, except that the cause remains untreated. The seat of disease is not the body at all, however, but the entire triune system of the person's body-mind-spirit entity. Few modern doctors will accept this as the basis for treatment. Cayce long held that the body is functional rather than structural. This means that the physical body is manifested or controlled by the underlying etheric body operating through the mind to "run" the physical outer body, which thus becomes a function of the etheric body.* Conventional medicine looks at the physical body as a structure of flesh and blood and deals with the mind as a separate instrument, though acknowledging that mind can indeed cause body to malfunction— or to heal itself.

To understand the work of bioenergetic healers such as Mr. Kolman, only the notion of humanity's triune nature can offer a scientifically acceptable explanation. No one need to look for the supernatural or for metaphysics to "explain" the miracle of their ministrations.

---

*The etheric body is a duplicate body within the physical outer body. It is made up of finer particles, and is also called the aura.

Mr. Kolman draws on the energy of his aura, the life force called bioenergy, which he has in abundance, and he ejects it in a controlled fashion through his sensitive hands. He also uses his psychic ability to see the patient's aura and his extrasensory perception to diagnose the problem to be dealt with. And that is all there is to the treatment.

PART ONE

1

Who Is
Ze'ev Kolman?

The purpose of this book is twofold: to share with you the extra-ordinary accomplishments of a great healer, a man currently prac-ticing his art for the benefit of those who seek him out, and to give an acceptable explanation of who he is and what happened to turn him into the healer he is today—in other words, to make sense of the Ze'ev Kolman phenomenon in practical but also scientific terms. The last thing I want anyone to do is to consider Ze'ev and his mission from a religious or even a metaphysical point of view. It would tend to obscure the hard facts and the veridicality of his results as a healer, and it probably would also weaken the burden of proof the world expects from someone whose work transcends the known. Our point of view, therefore, both yours and mine, must be objective but open-minded to the evidence presented, accepting as true only that which is seemingly supported by results, witnesses, and other forms of corroboration.

To understand this man and his mission amongst us, we should go back in time and reveal his early years and his development. Ze'ev was born in Tel Aviv on October 27, 1938, at six o'clock in the morning. His parents had emigrated to Palestine from Poland in 1935. There, they continued their interior-decorating business. Their religion was "standard" Jewish, not extremist or orthodox in any way. Ze'ev went to public schools and eventually joined in the family business. At age eighteen he was obliged to join the army. Although he recalled some threatening events in his life from age three on, there was nothing until age thirty-six that would suggest to him a career other than the one he was pursuing.

Ze'ev has painstakingly recalled his experiences of those early years. They were not particularly unusual or even interesting to anyone but himself and his immediate family, were it not for events that did not fit into the pattern of such an ordinary life. As we shall see, the events of his childhood, if properly understood at the time, would have foreshadowed coming events along similar lines. But to Ze'ev, even to his parents, the experiences that later helped shape his life and make it better understood were at the time puzzling, and it was beyond his ability to understand them or their origin, much less their meaning. Only in retrospect, as he considered the brushes he had had with death on several occasions as a child, did he realize that a higher power seemed to have protected him so later in life he could become what he has, in fact, become: Ze'ev Kolman, healer.

I see myself as a small child of about three standing on my bed in the middle of the night. It is the Second World War, and

Mussolini's planes are aiding the Germans by bombing Tel Aviv. It is pitch dark and I am standing on my bed, holding on to the bedpost and crying aloud for my mother to take me out of the bed to her arms. In the background the air-raid alarms are warning people to go down to the bomb shelters. All around there is the tremendous din of bombs exploding and buildings collapsing.

As a child of five, I experienced the fear of being killed through an event during the British presence in Palestine. The British army had military posts scattered about the country, both within the cities and outside of them. I remember standing in a street in Tel Aviv, not far from my home. A British soldier standing about idly at his post stretches out his hand and offers me a piece of chocolate, a very scarce commodity for us. He entices me to come closer, and seeing the chocolate I walk toward him. I am barefoot. Hesitantly and shyly I draw closer to the post, but the soldier, as his idea of a joke, left a live electrical wire on the sidewalk. My eyes are glued to the chocolate when my bare feet touch the open electrical wire. An electrical shock goes through my entire body. I am thrown into a brick wall.

The year is 1948 and I am nine years old. Egyptian planes bomb Tel Aviv. I am sitting on our porch. We live in a three-story building, and our apartment is on the ground floor. There suddenly is a continuous hum in the air, the sound of the propeller-driven plane getting ready to bomb the city. Then there is the sound of a massive explosion; a bomb has fallen on the house next to ours and has destroyed the entire side of the building. My mother shouts that we must run to hide in the bomb shelter, but the door to the stairway leading to it had been locked the previous night and in the confusion my father has forgotten where he put the keys. Then, suddenly, a massive explosion jars our building. The door to the stairway is blown off its hinges, acrid smoke fills the building, and the walls begin to sway from side to side. My mother takes hold of me and we manage to fight our way out of the house. The wire fence between the two buildings has been crushed. We reach the shelter of a neighboring building, and I burst into tears.

But the earliest psychic experience I recall vividly occurred when I was about five years old. My father was working in the Polish army camp in Israel at the time, a camp set up for people of Polish background. I accompanied my mother to the camp to see my father on one occasion, and being a lively child, I was running around the camp, playing. Suddenly, I fell and my chest hit a stake. I lost consciousness, and then I felt as if I were in a kind of mixer, swinging along back and forth through a tunnel. The tunnel was long, and inside the light was blue and purple. Then there was a silver light, and there at the gate stood my late grandmother, who had always been very close to me in life. She put her hand out in front of me and said, "My child, it is not your time . . . go back, go back!" Next thing I know, I am back between the camp tents; a soldier is talking to my parents.

A dramatic event occurred when I was about ten years old. The place was the courtyard. There are three citrus trees—a tangerine, a grapefruit, and an orange tree—and that courtyard has always appeared to me to be a bewitching and enticing paradise. The courtyard is lower than our building, and a stone wall about ten feet high separates the two courtyards. One day I climb the high fence and try to climb down into the mesmerizing Bienstock courtyard. As I climb down, I suddenly slip and take a nasty fall that leaves me flat on my back. Suddenly, within seconds, I find myself looking at my injured body from above lying there, while "I" am among the branches of the grapefruit tree. In these few seconds, my breathing has stopped. Only now do I understand that this was an experience of leaving the body as a result of physical trauma. In the few instants I think about my parents; I cry for the pain they will suffer because of me and cry among the tree branches—and all at once I "return inside." My physical body gets up off the ground and I begin to run home with whatever little strength I have left. Only as I begin to run does my breath come back to me. When I return home, I am shaken up and flustered, but, surprisingly, unable to complain about anything. I am completely sound; I have not suffered any injury and I do not feel any pain.

The last episode of survival occurred when I was a soldier in the army. At the time I was eighteen years old. As a new recruit, I am traveling in a truck packed with soldiers to a base in northern Israel. There we are to take an army course. It is nighttime, at the time of the Sinai Campaign of 1956. There are about twenty soldiers seated in the truck, and above us a canvas tarpaulin flaps in the breeze; we all doze off. The driver of the truck is especially tired, as he has not slept for a number of nights. In spite of his efforts to keep awake, he suddenly falls asleep at the wheel. The truck veers off the road and overturns in a wadi with a steep slope while we in the truck are thrown about as a giant mixer. Within those seconds I see death before my eyes. Instinctively, I allow myself to roll about and to fall along with the truck that is turning over, and I have an inner feeling that I am about to be crushed to death. The truck finally comes to halt. Everything becomes quiet, and I feel the tremendous weight of many kitbags as well as the spare tire, which is also inside the truck, all lying on top of me. There is a total silence in the dark. After a short check, I realize that I have survived, but within seconds I smell gasoline and I am suddenly afraid that the truck is about to burn and explode. With sudden, superhuman effort, I lift off the weight that has been pressing down on my body, and I run out of the truck with my remaining strength, alternately jumping and rolling on the ground in order not to be harmed by the imminent explosion. Nothing happens, and then in the dark I begin to hear the groaning of the wounded that are lying all around in that area. I again check myself and realize that *I am the only one* in the truck who came out of it without a scratch or injury. I was saved, I survived.

As I compare the developing years of the world's great seers, psychics, and healers, two peculiarities stand out in nearly all cases. First, the young person who eventually becomes an extraordinary individual possessed of special powers or, at least, abilities inevitably starts out among ordinary people in an average family and receives a realistic upbringing. Nothing in those early years indicates an unusual future—except for the second peculiarity. From time to time, otherwise inexplicable events occur in the youngster's life, events that usually puzzle, even frighten the young person and leave the parents either confused or sometimes downright hostile to the point that those events must somehow be explained away or ignored.

For more than thirty years, Ze'ev lived an ordinary life. Neither his family nor he had any inkling that he would have a very different future, different from the routine life he was leading. Had it not been for one night in 1974 and what transpired during the early morning hours following it, we would not have heard of Ze'ev Kolman, nor would this book have been written.

2

Encounter
on the Mountain

It is said by those who firmly believe in a well-ordered universe and destiny that everything happens at the right time and place, precisely when and where it is meant to occur. Although this begs the issue as to who determines these coordinates, I am inclined to agree with this view, based on long years of observation, research, and, yes, experience.

There comes a time when an event takes place that may forever change a person's life from that point onward. In Ze'ev's case, that moment arrived many years after his initial psychic encounters as a youngster and without any indication that something out of the ordinary was about to happen to him. To paraphrase an ancient dramatist, "A strange thing happened on the way to the mountain," and Ze'ev, the army-reserve soldier serving his stint in the armed forces, became a very different man.

I was thirty-six years old, on active reserve duty as I had been every other year. The plans for reassigning reserve soldiers had been changed, and I was sent, whether I liked it or not, to a military post in Sinai, a small post opposite the fortifications of Umm Hasheibah—a threat to Israel's security, as they were manned by the Egyptian army.

Our duty consisted of night surveillance. As it became dark, we would drive up in armored carriers to the lookout post at the top of a high mountain, and throughout the night we would watch the Egyptian position. At the end of our shift, before dawn, we would set out for our own camp, which was surrounded by a ring of hills. As we drove down, the camp would still be in total darkness while above us the day had begun to break.

The armored carrier led very slowly to the camp, which consisted of no more than a few tents. When we returned we would generally try to grab a few hours of sleep to make up for the hours we had missed.

One morning after we had arrived back at the camp, I went to sleep but awoke very soon, without knowing why and without being able to fall asleep again. It was about 6 A.M. when I left the tent for the open desert and gazed at the first light of the morning beginning to illuminate the camp. The air was clean and pure. I breathed deeply and went into the kitchen tent to drink a morning cup of boiling hot coffee. I stood outside the tent drinking the hot coffee while looking at the still desert view, whose beauty aroused a feeling of exaltation and amazement. I looked up at the mountain, to the lookout post on the horizon, and I suddenly felt a tremendous inner urge to climb the mountain alone while everyone in the camp was still fast asleep.

I left a note that I was climbing the mountain to the lookout post. This I placed in the kitchen tent, underneath my coffee cup.

I walked up slowly using the path that had been carved out to the lookout post above, feeling exhilarated and curious to know what could be seen in broad daylight from the vantage point which I knew so well at night. I felt fresh and not fatigued.

I reached the lookout post and saw the yawning abyss beyond the mountain which separated the place where I stood from the Egyptian position. From that altitude I had a bird's-eye view of everything below.

I was sitting on a rock, relaxing, when suddenly I noticed a bean-shaped structure, elliptic in shape. I stood up to see what it was, when the light—this structure—became even brighter and moved in my direction. There were hundreds of small projections coming from this thing, and as it came closer I felt the air being compressed and passing through me. Now this thing passed above my head at very fast speed, in the direction of Suez, casting a large shadow over the mountain.

Next thing I know I am surrounded by a kind of cloud, like cotton or sugar candy, and inside that cloud are eleven creatures, like human beings, standing around me in a half-circle. Their bodies were clear like milky glass; their heads were hairless; their eyes were outstanding; and as I watched in amazement, their faces seemed to reflect my own.

The white substance, the cotton candy, covered me now, and I felt completely powerless to act. A mixture of sounds came from their mouths, but I could not understand their language. Five of them stood on each side of me, and one was standing right in the center; he was of a darker color than the others and it seemed to me he was the leader. They were shorter than I was. They were standing partly on the ground and partly above the valley below.

Next thing I recall was my waking up from sleep and finding myself to my shock lying on my back at the edge of the mountain! I could not remember lying down on my back at all, or doing it at a spot where there were scorpions and snakes. I noticed it was already afternoon; the sun was now way down. I felt very dizzy and confused as to what had happened to me.

Suddenly I heard a metallic sound coming from the camp at the foot of the hill. As if from a deep sleep I looked down from the mountain, and below me stood a small, miniature camp, with the armored carriers and tents like boxes of matches. The sound was the beating of a metal bar on an armored carrier to alert me to come down and prepare for our night shift.

I knew I had seen these things, the figures had been there, and the events had indeed occurred.

I began to descend the mountain slowly in the direction of the camp. At this height it was still daylight, but the camp was already in darkness. With my emotions in turmoil, I could not tell anyone the experience I had gone through. I was afraid of becoming a laughingstock and firmly resolved not to speak about it to a soul.

When I reached the camp, I was greeted like a long-lost son. They were clearly alarmed at my disappearance and only then did I realize why. I had left the camp the previous night, in the early morning hours, and now it was already late afternoon. Clearly, there was missing time; most of it I could not, and still cannot, recall.

I went directly to the mess tent where the soldiers were sitting and eating. I went inside as if nothing had happened. Immediately after I came in, a soldier by the name of Eran came over and said something to me. I answered him absentmindedly and extended my hand. Eran took it and collapsed as if struck by lightning. Eventually, he opened his eyes, his face the picture of amazement. "Eran, how do you feel?" I asked. And he replied, "Fantastic."

The next few minutes were spent trying to calm down matters, and then another soldier came over and asked me to do for him what I had done for Eran.

Jokingly, I extended my hand and again the same thing happened—the soldier fell down unconscious. After that, a number of other soldiers also went through the same experience.

I would have regarded the whole thing as a joke but for the excitement it caused. For me, this phenomenon was very strange, even bizarre. At the time I had no knowledge or understanding of phenomena such as this.

The next morning I awoke from sleep at about 10 A.M., took a shower at the improvised camp shower, and returned to our tent. The tent contained eight beds, four on each side. On one of the beds, a soldier sat reading a book. I wanted to walk across the tent and to reach my bed at the end. The soldier put his legs across the aisle and refused to allow me to pass. I asked him to move his legs away, and he for his part asked me to climb over the bed from the side. As we were joking around, I decided to tickle his knees so as to move them. I did and the soldier suddenly sat up and began to scream, "You're electrocuting me! You're electrocuting me!" I laughed and continued to tickle him while he continued shouting. I didn't pay any attention to his words. He moved his legs away and I walked to my bed, laid down, and began to read.

The next day, when that soldier returned to the tent from the shower, he met me on the way and said to me, "Ze'ev, look at my knees . . . because of the electricity that you caused in me with your touch, the lesions on my knees have disappeared! For years hospitals gave me various ointments to apply, and yet the lesions never disappeared. . . ." Then he showed me the joints on his fingers, which were also red from lesions, and asked, "Would you possibly do the same for me here . . . with your hands?"

I took hold of the joints of his hands and murmured magic words from my childhood, something like "hocus-pocus." He again jumped backward and I thought it was all somewhat childish. To my amazement, he came back to me the next day and showed me the joints of his hands, which were totally lesion-free.

Yosef, one of the soldiers in our group, came over to me and told me that, each night, as it got dark, he would have tremendous headaches, and this had been going on for a number of years. He asked me—half-seriously and half in jest—to lay my hands on his head, for maybe that would offer relief to his throbbing head. I spontaneously placed my hands on his head and left them there for a time. He immediately told me that he had a pleasant feeling in his head, and, as he encouraged me to do so, I continued to lay my hands on his head. A few minutes later I took my hands off; he looked at me in astonishment and told me, "I feel tremendous relief. I feel great!"

A week later Yosef added, "Every night I wait for my headaches, but they no longer come."

By now I began to accept the strange things that were happening to me. From that day on, whenever we ascended the mountain at night, I spent long hours looking at the sky, concentrating on the stars overhead, turning my head over and over to the place where the strangers had appeared. Only once, at night, did I see something blinking like a large star that passed overhead from right to left and disappeared on the horizon.

I think that the figures neutralized all my actions in order to scrutinize me and to examine whatever they wished to. I believe that my body underwent a certain energetic process through the dense fog—the plasma which enveloped me—and through which my body must have absorbed something. Sometimes I feel a kind of thread which passes from my head through the length of my body—a thin silver thread. I remember that days after the event, when I looked at the palms of my hands, little silvery flakes appeared that I was able to scrape from my skin.

I understand that I was given the power of healing. Nevertheless, there are still many questions which remain unanswered: Who were those figures? Why and how was it "decided" to give me those powers? Why did they choose me? To this day these questions remain in my mind, and I cannot answer them. From this point of view, I feel like a utensil which does not know who created it and the loftier motives of its creator.

When I look back on my lifestyle at the time, I recall a humdrum life which was the exact opposite of my experience during that reserve duty. I was in my early thirties, just married and the father of two small children, and I ran a family business which sold curtains, carpets, and such for interior decorating. Most of my time was devoted to my work, except for hobbies, which included painting, sculpture, and, from time to time, writing poems.

The experience on the mountain left a deep impression on Ze'ev and, in fact, changed his life forever. To him, the encounter was beyond anything he had ever heard of, anything he understood or knew. But similar encounters have taken place before and after, and will most likely continue to occur. The question of why extraterrestrials—for that is what they surely were—make selective contact with human beings is a puzzling one seen from our point of view. But there are a number of well-known and properly documented cases of such encounters in the literature of UFO experiences, and many have been followed by extraordinary developments in the individual's psychic abilities or powers. It is also a fact that the majority of people who have this kind of experience are not skilled scientists or trained observers, but ordinary people who later become centers of attention because of their newly found abilities. It appears that these recipients of the extraterrestrials' attention are also carefully screened and selected and in many cases have shown inborn psychic abilities early on. This is certainly true of Ze'ev, but the extent to which his powers were increased by the encounter could not have been anticipated if it were not for the Sinai Desert experience.

Far from a religious or unique act of a Higher Power, the change of a somewhat psychic but ordinary individual into a world-renowned healer was a matter of careful mechanics. Whatever energy field the extraterrestrials placed around Ze'ev (he called it "like cotton candy"), it changed his bioenergetic potential. Because such experiences are not unique, I feel confident that what he reported did indeed happen precisely as he told it.

Ze'ev is not a religious man in the sense of being a fanatic. He is a spiritual person with a belief in a universal God, and his deep interest in the kabbalah indicates a certain involvement with mysticism. But he regards the incident on the mountain as tangible rather than visionary, and so do I.

The question remains: If these "people" he described (and his descriptions match those of many others who have had parallel encounters) turned an ordinary reserve corporal into a powerful healer, why did they do it? I don't think they are our "space brothers," as the fanatic fringe sometimes claims. I think this is part of an experiment on their part to see how changing a person like Ze'ev through their advanced biotechnology (the "cotton candy" cloud) would play out in the field of human beings. There are several cases which indicate that at least some of the humanoids visiting here are puzzled by our (less than perfect) physical bodies, and it may well be that this is all part of an experiment in terrestrial medicine jump-started by extraterrestrial biotechnology.

Only time will tell. It also means that Ze'ev would be monitored by those who made him a healer, and so it seems. On at least one occasion, at an international conference dealing with the preservation of the environment, Ze'ev had another encounter with his "friends" from Sinai, though this time he did not see their faces.

The facts concerning Ze'ev's ability to accomplish healing in many—not in all—instances, cases when often conventional medicine has failed, are undeniable. People will have less of a problem accepting this than they may have regarding the UFO incident that gave Ze'ev his new powers. Yet, belief and disbelief have nothing to do with evidence; we barely grasp the majority of happenings on our earth let alone the potential of other civilizations. It is therefore proper, and objectively scientific, to accept these events as true though unorthodox to many, because only then can Ze'ev's work and mission be properly understood.

3

A Unique
Kind of Healer

Through the years, I have had the opportunity to meet with and examine the work of unorthodox healing practitioners. I did this as part of my work writing about the paranormal in such a way that nothing important was overlooked or dismissed out of prejudice or sloppy research. I also looked with a jaundiced eye toward the delusive and frankly fraudulent.

As a result I met with the great English healer Harry Edwards at his healing sanctuary, where I experienced his healing touch, and I visited George Chapman, another eminent English healer, and again I felt great energy when he passed his hands over my body. Mind you, I did not seek their help for some incurable disease because conventional medicine had failed to offer a cure. I went as a researcher without prejudice one way or the other, alert and properly qualified to observe the procedure. Gordon Turner, a

London healer, worked on a minor ear problem and gave me relief, for a time, because I could not see him more often.

Edwards, Chapman, and Turner are gone now, and there are dozens of lesser lights I met and tested, both in the United States and abroad. In a current book entitled *Healing Beyond Medicine: Alternative Paths to Wellness*, I reported the exact impressions I received when undergoing treatments by these practitioners. Other healers of renown I tested were Ted Fricker of London, a simple man who heard a "voice" as a child telling him his mission was to heal, and the German medium Arthur Orlop, once a professional actor who eventually discovered that he could heal the sick.

I interviewed each healer in depth and required evidence to back up claims of accomplished results in the form of written attests by patient and doctor alike. Only then did I publish the healer's name, work, and where one could make contact. Then, Catherine, my wife at the time, and I subjected ourselves to the healer's hands, so to speak, carefully observing what we felt or noticed.

The people I investigated were neither frauds nor self-deluded; there was evidence of their successes, though not with every patient and not alike in each case. But sufficient data indicated to me the reality of the healer's powers to help the sick.

The conventional medical view is that healing outside medicine is by suggestion (and is thus self-healing), is somehow an inexplicable remission, or is due to misdiagnosis in the first place. This view is most convenient if we wish to avoid having to confront the possibility, nay, the probability of there being a system of healing outside conventional medical structure, particularly one that shows fully documented positive results. Only in recent years have a few medical doctors shown real interest in unorthodox healing methods, including, but not limited to, bioenergetic healing

Both patients and doctors care more about results that can be demonstrated, preferably permanently or at least of long duration, but patients are usually content with the results as they affect their well-being while doctors insist on knowing how it came about. But a system that requires two years or more to test a new drug or treatment before it is allowed into the mainstream of medical practice may take even longer to blend healing of this kind into the overall edifice of health practice.

Here and there paranormal healers work hand in glove with regular physicians for the benefit of all concerned, and some healers, like Dean Kraft, visit their patients in hospitals with the full cooperation of the attending physician. But that is, as yet, rare, even though truth often lies between two extremes—in Kraft's case the best of both worlds, conventional modern medicine and paranormal healing.

However, with some treatments or drugs, the two methods are at odds and cannot be reconciled in any way. For example, the approach taken by current mainstream medicine toward cancer treatment—radiation, chemotherapy—and that of the unorthodox medical practitioners and paranormal healers—stimulation of the body's own defense systems and bioenergetic healing—are not compatible.

Then there is the late Edgar Cayce, the seer of Virginia Beach, Virginia, who diagnosed illness when in full trance, at which time he also displayed an amazing array of medical knowledge he did not possess in the waking state. (He was a photographer.) Nor did he have an opportunity to "somehow" acquire this technical medical knowledge casually or inadvertently during his earlier years or by associating with doctors: a favorite explanation by those who would explain away anything sounding like a miracle or paranormal evidence.

(Curiously, Cayce, the prophet who predicted great changes in our world, was also a devout Baptist, and there is little doubt that his religious orientation colored some of those prophecies—to what extent remains to be seen.)

But Cayce giving a "reading" in trance was able to astrally project himself to examine "the body," as he put it, and to diagnose both illness and cause. At the same time, he offered a detailed cure using both known remedies and substances, and some unusual ones, frequently surprising medical doctors by his selections yet effecting cures by their use.

It is a moot point whence came this knowledge to "the sleeping prophet": was it spirit communication from The Other Side, perhaps by someone trained as a physician while in the physical state? Or was it superior knowledge from Cayce himself when in this trance state, somehow extending the boundaries of ordinary observation?

The fact remains: He did "read" thousands upon thousands of people seeking his help, and his advice, given in trance, worked wonders. The Cayce Foundation of Virginia Beach has published it all, including the prescriptions, so that people with similar ailments may also try them, now that Cayce has gone on.

But Cayce was so great a psychic and healer that no one remotely having his gift has emerged in the years since his passing in 1945. What has emerged, now and then, are claimants to his mantle: psychics, even amateurs with some psychic ability, purporting to have Cayce guiding them and speaking through them. From a woman in Connecticut to a couple in Cincinnati, Ohio, from a reader in Las Vegas to a healer in England—these people, not so much frauds as self-deluded, are as numerous as the postmortem fans of Elvis Presley who are convinced that The King communicates through them.

Nothing could be further from the truth, however.

To be sure, Cayce and his ways were unique and are likely to remain that way. But the results of his trance sessions in respect to healings accomplished can indeed be favorably compared to the results obtained by Ze'ev's bioenergetic healing. Ze'ev transcends the level of other healers, even those who use similar bioenergetic treatment methods, in the power generated by him through his hands and in the results, properly corroborated by medical authorities and witnesses.

Ze'ev is a relatively simple man, just as the most successful of healers and mediums are. Perhaps simplicity makes them better vehicles for the bestowal of that Great Power to heal; perhaps with simplicity there is less resistance to overcome, less ego to deal with, less to replace or push aside in the personality. Whatever the reason, it allows such people to devote all their energies to the healing work and not so much to other causes.

I have studied and tested Ze'ev and his work as a bioenergist, both on others he treats and on myself. As for his cases and their histories and evidence of healing, I will report on them in this work. As for myself undergoing his bioenergetic treatment, I know this: When Ze'ev moved his hands radiating bioenergy some ten inches above my body, I felt heat and a tickling sensation at the skin level.

I have felt it before with some of the great healers of the past—Edwards, Chapman, Turner.

I also felt the physical sensation of a gelatin-like field extending from Ze'ev's hands to the surface of my body, a tangible, touchable, quasi-material extension. Though invisible to the ordinary eye, it was there, connecting him to me as tangibly as if a towel had been extended from his hands to the surface of my body. When he held his hands close to my ear (in hope of reducing a tinnitus I have had for forty years), liquid appeared on his fingers and the ringing in my ear seemed lighter, at least for a while.

What Ze'ev has in his body, more than any of the others, is an enormously strong supply of bioenergetic energy, of life force, and he is able to project this force where it is needed through his hands. That, coupled with paranormal insight into his clients' problems, medical or otherwise, has convinced me that, indeed, Ze'ev is not like any other healer, past or present.

4

Understanding
His Gift

The event on the mountain had become the central theme of Ze'ev's life; he tried to understand what had happened to him, but he lacked a background that would allow him to come to grips with phenomena and experiences beyond what he had been used to in his life. Was this a unique experience or merely an incident of no further consequences? he wondered.

He was still in the military, and the daily routine took up most of his energies. But the events on the mountain would not simply fade away.

I came home one day on furlough. It was early afternoon when I opened the door to my house. I found it packed with people, and within a few minutes I understood that my wife, Miriam, who was a teacher by profession, was in the midst of a staff meeting which was being held in our home.

I walked in and was overcome by emotion, so that in the first few minutes of my meeting with Miriam I found it hard to stop the stream of words that flowed from me and quickly told her what I had experienced in Sinai. The words kept coming, and there I stood, still in my uniform with my rifle in hand, my body exhausted and sweaty.

I must have sounded confused. Miriam suddenly became alarmed and immediately thought that something had happened to me that had somehow damaged my rational thought processes. She sent me to shower while asking me not to say anything more in the presence of the teachers sitting there.

After the meeting ended we were free to talk leisurely, and I again told her everything that had happened to me: going up to the lookout post, the vision on the mountain I described as a great light, the return, Eran's fainting, and the healing of the soldiers. I tried to sound rational and convincing, but at the time she regarded me as confused.

In spite of this, the memory of the experience did not leave me. A few days later, I began to tell what had happened to me to close friends, including some who were doctors and psychologists; they were willing to listen, but their reactions were more or less the same. Each told me, in his own way, not to "delve into supernatural phenomena," because I would endanger my soul and my mental health. Again and again they suggested that I return to the reality with which I was familiar, and I, who was also inwardly afraid, listened to their advice and resolved not to deal with those events, and to leave them alone. In spite of this, the impressions those experiences had left were too strong for me to forget. I began to feel ill at ease. I needed guidance, and I asked for the names of people involved in supernatural phenomena. In the course of my investigation, I found out about a certain man known for his mystic pursuits. His name was Avshalom Drori. As someone who was naïve in such matters, I decided to contact him. I understood that his mystic pursuits were wide-ranging and that he concentrated primarily on hypnosis.

After a telephone conversation with him, he invited me to meet him at one of the halls where he used to lecture. I arrived at the meeting very excited, expectant, eager to understand what had happened to me. We sat down to talk, and I began telling him my story, even demonstrating to him some of the things I had done with the soldiers of my unit. Avshalom listened with interest. His main comment was that in his opinion I was not able to harm anyone, but, on the contrary, I was only able to help. He asked me if I was willing to assist people in general and mentioned the possibility of helping people who were drug addicts.

After that meeting Avshalom invited me a number of times to meet him, and at these times people began coming to me with various problems, all wishing to be aided through contact with my hands. Those who heard my story began to ask me for demonstrations and help, and they, in turn, sent me other people.

After a lecture I had attended, two young men came over to me; one of them introduced himself as David A. and told me that Avshalom Drori had sent him to me. The two accompanied me to my car and on the way told me David's problem:

he suffered from a bad stutter and unsightly distortions of the face and shoulders. They entered the car and I agreed to try to use my powers to help him. Sitting in my car, I passed my hands over David's head, above his face and his shoulders, and in a few minutes he felt relief and his face relaxed somewhat. From that time on David would frequently call me and would ask me for additional treatments in my home. After two or three months, his stutter ended totally and the distortions in his face and shoulder also vanished. But I did not know how the treatments worked. My techniques were experimental, as I passed my hands over the bodies of the people, above their heads, concentrating on their injured parts. My hands were always above the injured areas at varying distances, based on inexplicable feelings I had. In the palms of my hands there was a spongelike feeling, and I felt as if I was being guided by hidden forces to pass my hands at the correct distance from the injured area.

During that time my vision became sharper, and when I sat among people I began noticing, ever more clearly, an envelope of light, appearing somewhat like steam, around their bodies. Today I understand that this is an aura. I also became aware of this light aura during the treatments, and during the course of time I began to understand the changes that take place in it and to be able to understand the significance of these changes as guidelines for diagnosis and healing.

At that time also a young man named Danny came to me, his whole body covered with psoriasis, a skin disease with red, peeling lesions. Danny suffered as a result of this disease and among other problems found it difficult to make friends, to find employment, or to have an intimate relationship with a woman. I passed my hands over his body, and the next day, during a telephone conversation, he told me with great emotion that when he had gotten up in the morning he had found that the lesions were beginning to disappear. After a week he again called me and reported that the psoriasis was retreating constantly. He asked to come to see me again, hoping that he would be completely cured. I treated him a number of times after that, and the psoriasis disappeared as if it had never been. Danny found work and began to go out with women.

Two years later I heard from Danny again, when he told me that the psoriasis had begun to return, but much less severely. This time, too, my treatment worked, and since then I have not heard from him. The successes and the emotions which resulted from them made me happy and gave me the strength to continue helping others.

The treatments did not disturb the members of my family and were accepted with understanding, for on a day-to-day basis I continued to work in the store, our income was satisfactory, and life went on as usual. On the other hand, during this period my wife, Miriam, was still skeptical about the whole issue and regarded the treatments as purely random events that sometimes occur. She regarded me as the owner of a business and could not see me as a healer who would devote his whole life to this.

One day she returned from work at school, suffering from terrible back pains to the extent that she was unable to move.

She was in such agony that I tried to persuade her to see a doctor. After she refused, I sent for a private doctor to come to our home that evening. It so happened that this was a doctor who had needed my treatment in the past, and to my amazement he asked why did I not treat my wife myself. I told him that I did not know how, and in spite of his pleas, I refused to try.

That evening I called up a friend who was also a doctor and who suggested that I bring Miriam to the hospital the next day. During the course of that conversation, I asked his advice: Was it worthwhile for me to try to treat her before bringing her to the hospital? He explained to me that pain of that type generally continues for about three months, and he did not believe that I could help her.

In my heart I said to myself that even if I wouldn't help her, at least I wouldn't harm her, and I thus offered to treat her. She agreed and I began to try to use my powers. After the treatment Miriam got up from the bed, went into the kitchen, emotionally laughing and crying at the same time; the pain had disappeared, and the next day she returned to work at school. Since that event, her belief in my ability to heal others is firm and strong.

At that moment, Ze'ev knew that his life had, indeed, been changed forever and that there was no slipping back into complacency or a life of ordinary experiences and pursuits. He was determined to follow the new path that had so definitely opened before him, even though he failed to understand many things about it, including its origin and its direction.

5

A Full-Time Healer

Try as Ze'ev might, running the family business as he had before the incident in the Sinai Desert seemed not so satisfying anymore. Deep down inside, he knew that things had changed drastically. Somehow, people he did not know found their way to him.

About two years after the incident in the Sinai Desert, a strange old man entered our store. He introduced himself as Pinhas. He was tall with blue eyes, and he had a very high forehead. The skin on his face was smooth, almost unwrinkled. His face radiated light, and something about him elicited respect. He was dressed simply. He asked me if I my name was Ze'ev and then asked if he could steal a few moments of my time, and I agreed. We left the store together for the nearby square, where we sat down on a bench.

I asked him how he had come to me, and he mentioned the name of a person who had allegedly referred him to me, but I could not recall such a person. He then began to speak about energies and stated that there are positive and negative energies. He also claimed he had come to me because I had a great deal of power which he could see and feel, and he wished to help me. After that meeting the old man began to appear every week, each time on the same day, which was a Monday. Whenever he came to the store, time after time, he would apologize for having to steal some of my time. The store was generally packed, but I nevertheless left things as they were. Together we went out to hold our conversations on the same bench, in the same square.

In later conversation he told me about the great deal of knowledge which he had and about written material he wanted to give me to read. I refused to accept the material—I was afraid because I wasn't sure that I could read and delve into it and because I felt I didn't have the time.

Even though at that time I was not familiar with mysticism, I took his words very seriously. In my opinion, he was a spiritual teacher who came to me too early. One day he suddenly disappeared and never appeared again. I was evidently not ready yet to accept his words. At that time I was just beginning to understand myself and my powers.

Ze'ev did not want to turn his gift into a mystic talent, because he is basically a worldly, reasonable person, not in any way a religious fanatic or conformist. But the appearance of this stranger from nowhere did make him wonder about the future of his healing work: there had to be some sort of system, some kind of structure, to harness it. Then events forced his hand.

Meanwhile, the number of people who came to me began to grow significantly because of the rumors that had spread about my powers. On one occasion the principal of my wife's school approached her and asked if I could help her sick mother. She had heard vague rumors from one of the teachers in the school whom I had treated with my hands.

I consented to treat the woman, and after we had set up a mutually convenient time, we [the principal and Ze'ev] both went up to her apartment. When we came in, we were greeted by the principal's relatives while the mother lay helplessly on the couch, a blanket covering her body. I knew that she suffered from sharp lower back pains, and agony could be seen on her pale face. Everyone present looked at me tensely, impatiently, waiting to see what would happen. The mother also scrutinized me.

Within a few minutes, I went over to the sofa upon which the mother lay and began to treat her, concentrating intensely. In those minutes the principal felt tremendous curiosity to know what was happening as I moved my hands, and without realizing it she moved over to me. Without warning, she suddenly placed her own hands between the palms of my hands in order to try to feel the energy I had. Instantaneously, she was forcefully flung away from the area as if she had received an electric shock. She was actually thrown a few yards. But nothing happened to her, even though she had fallen, yet the tremendous shock of energy left her speechless.

One morning a friend called me and told me about an acquaintance of hers who had asked her to contact me on her behalf. "I am calling," she said, "for a woman named Mrs. Robbins, who has just arrived from England. She is now at the Moriah Hotel and has a strange story to tell."

Mrs. Robbins had undergone an operation on her abdomen eleven years earlier, and as a result her left hand had swollen to insufferable dimensions, to the extent that the fingers had become permanently closed. In addition, the scar from the operation had not healed properly, and ever since it had kept oozing matter, causing her great and continuous distress.

Mrs. Robbins explained how she had visited some of the greatest doctors in Europe in the past few years and had even traveled to the United States to find a cure. None of the doctors had managed to ease her suffering. After she had returned to England, she had a strange dream. In the dream she was told to visit the Holy Land, where she would be cured, not by a doctor but through unconventional means. The dream disturbed her greatly, and as a result she had decided to travel to Israel. Now she was at the Moriah Hotel in Tel Aviv. Simply by chance Mrs. Robbins told her story to the saleslady in the souvenir shop at the hotel, and it was the saleslady who had heard from her friend about a man who would fit the dream. Hence my friend's call to me.

That same night I drove to see Mrs. Robbins at the home of that friend. When I entered the house, Mrs. Robbins was sitting on a sofa in the living room with her left hand resting on the armrest. She was wearing a short-sleeved dress, and a shawl over her shoulders hid her hand. When she removed the shawl, I shuddered at what I saw, for the hand was so grossly swollen that one cannot describe it in words. I began to treat her. I concentrated deeply and went into a trance state. During the treatment the hand of the patient suddenly started turning red, and Mrs. Robbins turned to me and cried out, "The hand is warming up . . . the hand is warming up . . . ! Move your hands away from it a little!" The hand kept becoming more and more red and remained in that condition after I completed the treatment.

The next day the souvenir saleslady contacted me; I was tense and listened intently. "Mrs. Robbins," she said, "is standing next to me, but she is afraid to talk, she is so overwhelmed and moved." When Mrs. Robbins woke up in the morning, she looked at her hand and noticed that there were small lesions on the back of it. As she picked at them, one of the lesions opened up and a stream of blood gushed out. A few minutes later, Mrs. Robbins began to move her fingers. When she examined her body, she found that the scar on her abdomen had closed completely.

After she had calmed down, Mrs. Robbins asked to see me again. At her request, I treated her a number of times after that, until her hand was completely healed.

One day a man who introduced himself as Rabbi Zimroni from Bat Yam contacted me and told me that he had heard about me from the Habad Hassidim community in Holon, my hometown.* He told me on the phone about a young man named Michael who was a cancer patient in the Tel Hashomer Hospital. The doctors had given him only four more days to live. Michael was sixteen years old and a student of Rabbi Zimroni at Yeshiva Hadar Hatemimim. He asked me to come to the hospital and treat the youth.

The next morning Rabbi Zimroni and Michael's father, Aryeh, came by car to take me to the hospital. As we drove, Aryeh told me that Michael's condition was critical. He was doubtful if it was even possible to help the child, because for a number of days the doctors had been predicting that death was imminent.

We arrived at the hospital, and the three of us walked toward the building where Michael lay, Building 25, where he was housed in an isolation room. As we entered the room, I was astonished to see that it was packed with people, some of them rabbis dressed in long black coats. They were murmuring quietly, praying incessantly as they all crowded around the youth's bed. Next to the bed sat Michael's mother, and she periodically moistened the youth's lips.

Before me was a young man, terrifyingly thin, stretched out on the bed. His bones protruded through his pale and semi-transparent skin. His face was thin and yellow, his eyes large and pleading for help.

Rabbi Zimroni introduced me; all were already aware of who I was and expected me. For a moment the group made

*Hassidim are communities of ultra-orthodox Jews who live outside the mainstream of both Judaism and the world around them.

room for me so that I could approach the bed, but immediately the circle closed about me again. I looked at the aura around Michael's body, and only with difficulty was I able to make out that it was still there. In spite of my fears, I passed my hands over his body and with great concentration began to transfer my energies to his body.

Immediately after the treatment, Michael said in a weak voice, "Mother, tell father to help me get up . . . I want to eat something, to drink something." His mother was moved to tears. She grated an apple for him, added honey, and fed him. Afterwards he drank orange juice, and it appeared as if an inexplicable force of renewal had begun flowing in him. I looked around me and was surprised to notice tears in the eyes of the people. They explained to me that Michael had been fed intravenously throughout the entire time, and that for two weeks he had not eaten a thing. He was also receiving a morphine injection every six hours, for he was in constant excruciating pain.

Michael began to regain strength. In the following days I visited him a number of times, and a few days later he was taken off his bed and brought to the hospital cafeteria to eat. Now he only needed morphine injections every sixteen hours. After ten days Michael was taken in a wheelchair to the wedding of relatives. The frequency of my visits began to decline as Michael got stronger.

One day, very early, Aryeh, Michael's father, called me, and in a voice choking with pain said to me, "Don't ask what happened to Michael . . . You have to come very fast . . . I am coming to take you to Michael as fast as possible."

When I asked him, alarmed, what he meant, he answered, "I will tell you everything that happened on the way to the hospital . . . It's a waste of valuable time now . . . I'm on my way to you."

In a few minutes he was at my house, and only on the way to the hospital did he tell me that the doctors had wanted to give Michael chemotherapy. Aryeh had mentioned that he opposed this, and when he refused to permit the treatment, the doctors claimed that hospitalization was then valueless. Furthermore, unless he was treated Michael would be discharged from the hospital and sent home. The family was extremely afraid to take Michael home and therefore agreed that he be given the chemotherapy.

When we arrived at the hospital I found Michael in critical condition, as he had been when I first saw him. He was lying in bed; almost all his hair had fallen out, and his *peyot* (sideburns) were very thin. The bed cover and the pillow had hair on them, for it kept falling out.

When he realized that I had arrived, he looked at me pleadingly with his large and prominent eyes and called out to me in a broken voice, "Ze'ev . . . save me! Save me. . . ." I felt terrible. I came close to him and tried to soothe him, but was unsuccessful. Michael continued groaning and said that he felt that his whole body was burning and in pain. He twisted and turned constantly because of this pain, and when I saw the great amount of suffering that he was going through, I used all my power in a desperate effort to pass my hands over his body. I tried to direct the waste in his body to the lower regions of the body and the soles of his feet, and from there outside the body. To my surprise, the pain ceased and Michael calmed down. Aryeh took me back to my home.

The next day, though, Aryeh called me and told me that Michael's pain had evidently moved to the soles of his feet, and he was suffering excruciating pain in the soles. Again we drove to the hospital, and then, on the way, something very strange happened. Without my planning to do so, I began to give Aryeh directions, the main point of these being that he was to take sterilized needles and to prick Michael on the soles of his feet at the places that I would indicate. An inexplicable force came from within me at the time; the words were not my own.

When we arrived, Michael's mother sat at his side, and Aryeh told her what I had said. She left the room and returned within a few minutes carrying sterile needles, cotton wool, and alcohol. She asked me to do what I had recommended.

With a heavy heart, I began to cleanse the yellow soles of Michael's feet with alcohol. Afterwards, I pricked them at the points that I understood were the important ones. The pricks were light and did not draw blood. As I treated him, the pain disappeared, as if it had never been present. Later, in retrospect, I realized that by doing what I did I had opened the energy blockage in the soles of his feet.

A few days later, Aryeh contacted me again and asked me to come. On the door of the room in which Michael lay was a picture of Rabbi Schneerson, the illustrious Lubavitcher Hassidim Rebbe in Brooklyn, New York. At the time I was about to travel to the United States because I had been invited to the rebbe's "court." Michael knew about my trip to the Lubavitcher Rebbe, and he had expressed his desire to join me on my trip.

I started to treat Michael, sending energies into his body, moving the palms of my hands downward and then upward. Suddenly, as I was concentrating deeply and passing over Michael's body with my hands, I felt a tremendous force pulling me from him. I was thrown to the door and hit the portrait of the rebbe as I swayed uncontrollably.

Michael became frightened and asked, "Ze'ev . . . what happened? What happened? Did you lose your balance?" I answered that that was the case, but I did not want to tell him what I had felt in the split second that I had been detached from him: It was at that instant that I realized my mission to help him, as I had been doing for the past four months, had come to an end.

About two days after this episode, Aryeh called. "Ze'ev, Michael asked that you come. He wants to see you. He does not want treatment. He only wants to see you."

When I arrived at the hospital, I realized that Michael's condition had deteriorated drastically. He lay on the bed with eyes closed, his mouth half open, his tongue cracked and yellow. He was in a deep morphine daze. I went over to him, patted his head, and said, "Ze'ev is here . . . you hear me." He looked at me for a few seconds and then his eyes closed.

I felt terrible, sad, and helpless.

In October of 1981, I traveled to New York to see Rabbi Schneerson, the Lubavitcher Rebbe. I had been invited to his court, and to spend the Sukkot festival with him after his Hassidim had written to him about my treatments. At the time I had treated a number of Lubavitcher Hassidim in Holon. After a great deal of hesitancy on my part, I had been persuaded to make the trip.

When I drove to Ben Gurion Airport, I found to my surprise that not only had my immediate family come to see me off, but many Hassidim had also come to accompany me. Not only that, but when it came time to get on the plane, the Hassidim escorted me, dancing!

I arrived in the United States on a Friday morning. My hosts were the Roth family, whose hospitality throughout was exemplary. That day I arrived at their home and rested.

On October 24, I was on my way to the rebbe's office next to the synagogue, on Eastern Parkway in Brooklyn. Suddenly, a Hassidic man passed by and asked if I was the man who had treated Michael. At that instant I was convinced that Michael had died. It was 1:00 P.M.

The next morning as I sat in the synagogue, one of the Hassidim, the son of Rabbi Lande of B'nai Brack congregation, came over and told me that he had something to tell me. I answered that he no doubt wanted to tell me that Michael had died the previous day at 1:00 P.M. New York time. He froze where he stood and asked, "How do you know?" With a heavy heart, I told him.

Another week passed and I was now invited, together with a number of other people, to meet with the rebbe in his office. We all walked to the office together. When we entered, I saw a medium-sized room packed with books, with the rebbe sitting bent over his desk. The room was illuminated by the autumn light which entered through a large window. He began to speak, blessing me and the others. In speaking to me directly, he told me that it was my duty to heal the sick. He also mentioned that in Israel I would meet a "rabbi who issues rulings," but at the time I did not understand what he meant. I received his blessing to close our store in Israel and devote my time to healing. I returned to Israel. In my hand was Rabbi Schneerson's written request to meet with the rabbi who issues rulings in Israel.

Even though Ze'ev was not an orthodox Jew, but considered his religion from the secular point of view, he knew that the Lubavitcher Rebbe was held in high esteem in Israel. The rebbe was considered the Messiah by his devout followers and, to some, a man who could bring about miracles. Perhaps the fact that Ze'ev, too, had worked "miracles" in healing Michael for a long time had induced the rebbe to invite him. Michael's death, after all, was the work of misguided medical doctors; otherwise, Ze'ev's work would have indeed saved him. For Ze'ev it was then, as it is indeed now, important to be considered not a faith healer but a scientifically valid bioenergetic healer whose work could be verified and tested in a nonreligious environment. Still, he did not wish to offend the rebbe who had blessed him.

Some time later, the Lubavitcher Hassidim introduced me to Rabbi Lande of B'nai Brack, who had heard about me after a number of people in his congregation had been treated by me. Rabbi Lande, as it were, reinforced the words of the Lubavitcher Rebbe and as his emissary "ordered" me to close our thriving store and to deal only with the sick. I was not able to make such a momentous decision so fast. As an interim solution, one of the Hassidim enabled me to work in a clinic in Givatayim, a city close to Holon.

Emotionally, I was not ready to close the store. Many people came to the clinic, but I could not demand any payment for the treatments. I earned my living from the store.

There is a side to Ze'ev's character that embraces the mysticism of the kabbalah, and he has good reason to take psychic experiences, even of the most incredible kind, seriously—after all, they happened to him! But the realistic, scientifically oriented side of his personality did not cherish the idea of becoming a religious guru, a person to be worshipped because he could heal. What Ze'ev cared about were rational explanations for his gift, and he has kept those two approaches separate. He considers the visit with the Lubavitcher Rebbe and the Brooklyn Hassidic community an honor—but perhaps it was the other way around: Did the rebbe come after Ze'ev because of his success as a healer to bring him into their fold?

Before Ze'ev could properly evaluate the Hassidim's motive in contacting him, events took decisions out of his hands. This mystic eighteenth-century cult, offspring of traditional Judaism but following extreme ways, was not going to dictate what he should do with his gift of healing. But the people who needed him made that decision for him.

As I was involved more and more with healing, the store began to suffer. I decided that I had to restore it to its former position and therefore devoted more time to it, and it began to function as it had done previously.

As I was spending more time in the store, a steady flow of people began coming to it, searching for me to help them. They would come from morning to night seeking relief for their diseases. I asked them to come to a certain hall that had been given me by Lubavitcher Hassidim and to donate money to charity for the treatments received. In spite of my request, the store filled up more and more with sick people; there was disarray inside the store.

About a year after I had visited the Lubavitcher Rebbe, I was offered a place to work in a medical clinic in Tel Aviv that dealt with Eastern medicine. At first I turned down the offer, as I still felt that I could not close down a business that had flourished for forty years. But eventually I did close the store, and it has stood empty ever since.

I worked at this clinic for about a month. From it I moved to another clinic in Netanya, a city close to Tel Aviv, and in the end decided to open my own clinic, close to our home in Holon.

When Ze'ev started work in his clinic, the searching phase of his life came to an end. He had accepted his mission without further hesitation and was ready to serve the world. No longer could he provide healing treatments as a hobby: it had become his full-time occupation, and that was how he would earn his living henceforth. He hesitated at first, but then he recalled the words of a Belgian rabbi he had met through his encounter with the Lubavitcher Rebbe in New York. The Belgian rabbi, when hearing of Ze'ev's healing work and his quandary about accepting payments for his services, had shaken his head. Services performed without proper compensation aren't worth much, he had advised Ze'ev. To this day, however, Ze'ev will provide free treatment for certain people who are unable to pay. But the majority will pay for his treatments. It is, for better or worse, human nature to value things according to what they cost.

The surprise blessings of the Lubavitcher Rebbe were not the only indications that Ze'ev had been plucked from obscurity to become one of the modern world's great healers. Not one to become overawed by his accomplishments and to this day puzzled by some aspects of it, Ze'ev nevertheless received a very strange kind of "endorsement" in 1988 that proves both his chosen status and his ability to have psychic experiences of the most complex kind.

Early in the morning on August 30, 1988, he was awakened from deep sleep by a strange feeling of a presence.

My wife was still asleep at my side, but when I looked to the right I noticed near my head the figure of a thin, erect man. His face was wrinkled, and he wore a gown called *galabia*; his head was covered by a Moroccan cap. His eyes were very clear as he stared at me. Instantly, I recognized the man even though we had never met, but I had heard stories about him. He was a holy man named Baba Salim, and people were coming to him for healings for many years. One of the things he was famous for were his bottles of blessed water, which he passed out to those seeking his help.

I knew, of course, that the Baba had died two years prior to his visit with me. People often prayed at his gravesite. As I lay there in bed, completely shocked at what I perceived, the apparition kept on gazing at me intently. He looked as real as a physical person. But then he began to move, slowly, from near my head down to my feet. Then he opened his mouth and spoke to me. "I am traveling abroad from time to time, and I have a lot of spare time."

I kept thinking, How could an old man like this travel so much? when I realized again that he had died. He stopped near my stomach area now and took a small bottle from beneath his gown. Immediately, I recognized the bottle. It looked exactly like an identical bottle which had been given to me many years before by a man named Menahem, a healer who used oil to heal people, and this was one of the bottles he had used. The bottle contained oil for healing, and I decided to use it at a future occasion. It so happened I was then giving healing treatments to a man by the name of Kaminsky who was suffering from neuroma pains from an amputated leg, phantom pains even though the physical leg was gone. During one of my treatments, I spontaneously decided to try the oil in the little bottle, but it slipped from my hands and broke into tiny fragments.

Now here was the same bottle, whole again by some miracle. Only this time it was empty. The Baba put the bottle into the folds of the blanket that covered me in bed, saying, "Take the bottle, fill it with water, and give it to your sick patient—he will recover!"

Then, waving his hand he moved toward a cupboard in the room and faded into it. In a moment he had completely disappeared. I realized then that this great healer had come to me from the Great Beyond to encourage my work as a healer, too.

6

Understanding
His Powers

Ze'ev had finally realized he was different from most people, even from other healers. But he still did not quite understand the mechanics of his powers, only the likely results. For a man who had grown up as an average citizen and ordinary businessman in Israel, the concept of auras and chakras was rather revolutionary. Yet he eagerly explored the energies he had been given.

Gradually, he began to accept the situation as real and even normal in terms of bioenergetic healing. But, like a latter-day Alice in Wonderland, he was astonished by it all, even more so than were the people he helped. At no time did he assume that he was a genius or a guru, somehow outside natural law. To the contrary, he sought early on an explanation for the seemingly "super" natural ability to see people's problems and deal with them, not derived from acquired knowledge, but from outside himself. He sought those answers not in traditional religious belief, with all its pitfalls, but in a higher, spiritual order of which he had become a part.

Ever since I began to treat and heal people, I have always thought that somehow or other I am being directed, in a way that I cannot understand or explain. One day I treated a certain Dr. A. C., who had been operated on to remove a growth from his leg. Under my treatment, the incision healed completely within two days. Dr. A. C. and I became good friends, our friendship continuing to this day. Sometime later, Dr. A. C. called and told me that a friend of his, Dr. Gideon Ron, was in contact with a famous medium from Britain who was now visiting Israel. Dr. A. C. invited me to Dr. Ron's clinic in Rishon-le-Zion for a social evening, to which he invited various doctors who were acquaintances of his and of Dr. Ron. Also invited was the British medium Ursula Roberts. Ursula Roberts had no prior knowledge of my being present. While she was in a deep trance, one of the doctors went over to her, pointed to me, and asked if she was able to say anything about me. Miss Roberts pointed at me and said in a dramatic tone, "He's a healer!"

The doctor continued, "Do you see his spirit guides?" Her answer was again dramatic and unequivocal. "Yes, his guide is an Indian doctor from North America." Her words were surprising, but didn't move me, because at the time I was not aware of the concept of spiritual guidance. But I have always loved Indian art motifs and the Indian lifestyle. For some reason I have always felt an inexplicable connection to Indian folklore as a whole.

As time went on, I realized that much of the intuitive treatments I was giving were in reality the product of assistance which came to me from sources outside myself. At one point I was able to see the entities which guided my work. They looked like transparent figures or shadows with faces and appeared behind the backs of those I was treating, standing between the patients and the walls of the treatment room. Eventually, over a long period of time, I was able to name the entities and to predict when they would appear. For example, I learned that different types of entities appear to different kinds of people during the healing, although all the entities are linked to me. In other words, I understood that every person receives the spiritual support which is appropriate for him. I also began to sense other entities joining the treatments I was giving. Among them, for example, there are three figures of zaddikim.* Sometimes two of them appear, while other times all three are present. These, too, have been seen by some of my patients. I have noticed that the zaddikim, for example, appear when I treat religious Jews. In such cases, the Indian doctor entity does not appear. As opposed to this, other entities appear when nonreligious people come for treatment. As I understand it, the aid I receive which enables me to treat others comes from two sources: The first of these are various spiritual beings who are physically alive today. Their spiritual

---

*Zaddikim or holy men, not unlike Christian saints, occur in many world religions, from Indian avatars to Tibetan ascended masters. They are the spirits of advanced human beings, not supernatural entities who never walked the earth, as some would have it.

presence offers me assistance during the treatment. They seem to "appear" when I ask for their aid and when I am in a deep state of concentration. One of these was the Lubavitcher Rebbe, while he was alive, I am convinced. Assistance also comes to me from the entities not in their physical bodies, such as the three zaddikim and the Indian doctor.

In my work today, I feel the presence of my spiritual guides when I begin treatment. The contact is very intuitive, and the first thing I feel is a stream of energy which enters through my shoulders and neck, as if a body had superimposed itself on my own, and then the energy flows through my hands. I compare this energy to two rods of light of about fifteen inches in length and about two inches in width, which are gripped by me and radiate powers to the person being treated. In the region of the so-called third eye in my forehead, I feel an extremely concentrated ray of light, like that of a laser. The healing will then take place, provided the body of the patient is ready to absorb the energy and provided that it is in keeping with the personal karma of the individual. Personally, I do not see my spiritual guides during the treatments, but I sense them. In many other cases, though, when I am sitting at ease in my room or when I tilt my head to the side purely by chance, I see their presence about on the walls of the room, but just for a few seconds.

One evening in 1982, I was invited to lecture on spiritual healing at a public hall, Beit Remez, in Netanya. There were eighty people present, and I was due to take my place in the program immediately after one Dr. Menasheh Eini. When I rose to speak, I began by making a number of remarks about bioenergy, the force with which I am able to heal. As I spoke I suddenly noticed that some of the members in the audience were not listening to me at all, but people seated in front of me were whispering to one another and pointing at me in amazement. I was unable to continue with my lecture and asked what was happening. The members of the audience then told me that behind me, against the white wall, they were seeing the misty outline of three entities. The majority of the people present had no idea who or what these were, while a small minority of the audience realized that these were the three holy men with beards. I calmed everyone down and told them that these figures were familiar to me. That night the figures were evidently directing me in my speech. Frieda Fogel, a parapsychologist, was present in the hall that evening, and I remember her in one of the front rows facing me. She described her experience of that night in Netanya as follows:

"During the speech, someone grabbed me forcibly and asked, 'Frieda, is what I am seeing correct? Is it correct?' And indeed, behind the figure of Ze'ev there were the images of his spiritual guides—three figures with beards in white robes, with the heads somewhat indistinct. There was confusion. People did not understand the phenomenon they were seeing. A number grabbed me by the hand and said, 'Do you see? Do you see?'"

The entities of the zaddikim seen in Beit Remez were also seen by one of my patients in one of our sessions in my clinic. Here is the way Smadar A. described it:

"The second time I came to Ze'ev, literally in the middle of the treatment I suddenly saw behind his head a shining pear-shaped object of a golden color, which I later realized was the aura behind his head. I was astounded. Afterwards I asked Ze'ev what was going on and what exactly I was seeing. He responded that I was seeing his aura, and he explained that auras such as this are to be found around every person's body—just as there is one around my own body.

"Suddenly, three images of small people appeared at the side of Ze'ev, looking like negatives; one appeared above and disappeared, immediately afterwards the second appeared underneath, and when it disappeared the third appeared. I was so amazed that I remained speechless. To the best of my recollection, the entities appeared as black-and-white pictures. They had beards and I think they wore cloaks, but I am not sure of that because everything happened so fast. In size, these entities were even smaller than Ze'ev's face, and after they appeared, they just looked at me and disappeared."

A young woman named Navah Ruhan came to my clinic. She was about thirty years old, a housewife without any specific outside occupation. She came as she suffered pain throughout her body. "I went into Ze'ev's room and sat in a chair, very tense; my whole body felt like lead. Ze'ev then passed his hands over my legs, over my hands, with movements which caused me to feel something like electric current, and I felt relaxed. Ze'ev asked if anything was hurting me, and I answered that he had to find out for himself. He then passed his hands over my entire body, without touching. He then said to me, 'There is something in the abdomen and something in the neck.' I was totally flabbergasted, because I suffer from hypothyroidism and have a hernia, and I was to undergo an operation. He defined the places exactly. He then began the treatment. I saw at his right side some type of shadow which moved. It was something blurred, like a figure in the fog, and I was amazed: right next to him stood an Indian, aged between about eighteen and twenty-two, a young man with a quiver full of arrows on his back, with some type of stick under his left armpit and a case of sticks in his right hand, like golf clubs. I described to him [Ze'ev] what I saw."

As time went on, I devoted more and more of my time to the study of these shining light fields [auras], and my vision became clearer. Gradually, I was able to see them whenever I wished. I noticed a great range of colors and shades within them. I noticed how they changed from one situation to another, such as before and after bioenergetic treatments or with people's changing moods. Similarly, I learned from long and patient observation to identify, within these auras, signs of disease or blockages of energy.

The aura field envelops our bodies like a three-dimensional bubble, and it is generally most visible around the head, down to the shoulders, and around one's hands. I have learned to differentiate three major layers of the aura. I refer to the first layer of the aura as the small layer, as I see it between about half an inch to an inch from the person's head and body. This layer supplies me with information on the person's health, his emotional state at that moment, and his general spiritual level. The most common colors of this layer are white, light blue, yellow, orange, gray, and dark blue. When a person is healthy, the aura is shiny, clear, and vital. A gray and murky aura shows me that the person is ill, and if the aura is especially gray, it shows that the person's days are numbered.

When the energy in a person's body is balanced, the aura appears symmetrical on both sides of the body. There are, though, conditions where the aura appears only on one side of the body while it is nonexistent or very weak on the other, and that shows an imbalance of energy. Successful bioenergetic treatment immediately brings about noticeable changes in the aura. It begins to shine, and its colors become brighter and clearer. The vitality of the aura is also expressed in its size, so that in the case of a healthy person the aura will be much larger than that of a person who is ailing. I found that a person's feelings and state of mind are reflected in the small aura. When a person becomes excited, his aura turns yellow, grows, and expands in height until it fades out and leaves a kind of yellow blotch in the center of the aura. Basic emotions such as joy, anger, sorrow, tension, and love are visible in the aura. Joy is shown by a blue aura, whereas tension, sorrow, and hurt result in a yellow aura. Anger and tension are sometimes expressed in yellow or green blotches in the aura, while green indicates blockages of energy and disquiet in the person. A milky white color mixed with blue indicates the presence of feelings of love. Sleeping plays a significant role in cleaning the small aura and in purifying it of the impressions made on it during the day. Over the years I noticed that the condition of the aura changes drastically before and after the night, and I understood that a person goes to sleep with an aura loaded down with waves of colors and emotional blots which were received during the course of the day. As the soul undergoes a refining and purifying process during the night, the energy field around the body undergoes a type of filtering and cleaning, so that the following morning the aura appears to be white or blue and generally shines.

Spiritual healing purifies the emotional energies in the patient's aura. Often when I look at a person who has come to me, as he sits down across from me I see his aura in different colors changing rapidly, and I believe that this stems from the person's fears and expectations of his visit with me. At that time the aura is in a state of confusion: the colors are diffused and less defined or clear. However, once I create the first contact with the patient, sometimes even in a matter of seconds the person calms down and then the energies are directed into their proper channels, and the colors of the aura become differentiated and clear. Only then am I able to examine and diagnose the aura as it naturally is.

Other information can also be derived from the colors and the radiation of the small aura, such as the level of spiritual development of the individual. I have seen the aura of a criminal as dark blue and muddied. People who are moral within the accepted norms, without any special talents or a specially spiritual life, will radiate a clear white light or sometimes pale blue. The aura of specially spiritual people is seen by me as a clear, pure violet.

I refer to the second layer of the aura as the large layer. The size of this aura varies from between two to twenty inches, the average being four to six inches. The higher and larger the aura, the better the person's mental and vital health. This aura appears to me like a small panoramic screen in which I can also find information about the person's past and present, pictures from his previous incarnations; this information often relates to the reasons for the person's illness in the present life. Signs of local disease appear in the large aura as colored stains in the shape of bean-shaped figures. A reddish stain on the left side of the ear relates to a problem in the liver; the darker the color (red or orange), the more severe the affliction. Signs of other diseases appear in the form of blurry blotches of various shades of muddy blue or yellow, or sometimes as "holes," or areas without energy. These energy holes appear in the aura above the specific organ affected.

The broad aura, which appears beyond the large aura, relates exclusively to spiritual visions, entities which accompany the person, or pictures related to the future. In the spiritual realm the concepts of time, movement, and place do not exist. The panoramic field of the large and broad auras, in which I see pictures, is only revealed to me to the extent the person across from me permits it. Some people can, by the force of their will, close off this field.

The bioenergetic treatments I give take place in the aura and permit the flow of beneficial energies into their bodies, opening energy hubs. These energy hubs are known as chakras, and the lines of energy flowing in the body are known as meridians.

The ability to see these began soon after the Sinai Desert incident and during my army reserve duty, in Ein Yahav, near the Dead Sea. One of the soldiers complained about terrible pains in his kidneys; he was due to be examined by the doctor the following day. He had been suffering with kidney stones for some time, and they caused him excruciating pain. I asked him to lie down on the bed. I then began to concentrate on his kidneys, and I suddenly saw a small, round shaft of light above his abdomen. I began to pass my hands over the area. Suddenly, I became aware of other small shafts of light in the upper regions of his body, their color being bluish white. I noticed a number of others: on the head, in the middle of the forehead close to the eyebrows, on the neck, at the heart, and at a point below the soldier's abdomen. As it was the afternoon and the light that entered the solitary window in the hut was very weak, I first thought that this sight was stemming from my desire to help the soldier and was distorting my vision. I asked the soldier if he, too, saw this. He looked at me suspiciously, peered at the places I had mentioned, and said that he saw nothing. I again looked at his whole body from head to toe, and suddenly I saw, in addition, thin strands of light beginning at the soldier's head and joined together, finally reaching the area of his legs. Thus, his entire body shone from those thin, shining strands and from the shiny hubs to which they were connected. I continued to pass my hands over his body, from head to toes, and concentrated on the region of the kidneys. The soldier told me that he felt as if static electricity were coursing through his body. He relaxed and allowed the treatment to take its course. After a number of minutes, he suddenly gave a big groan and reported a sharp pain in the region of his kidney. I felt that

I had to end the treatment, and the soldier himself felt that he had had enough. Two hours later the soldier came over to me and reported that when he went to urinate, small stones began to be passed as well. There was a burning sensation and a little blood. The stone had been crushed into small fragments which had been evacuated from the kidneys.

When I examine a person, it is easier for me to see the chakras when the light is dim, almost dark. I notice their size and the colors that appear in them. The appearance of the aura changes as the circumstances change, and the same is true for the chakras, which change their appearance in various physical and emotional situations. When a person is open, relaxed, and healthy, the chakras appear to be open in a remarkable way: they are large and appear broad and occupy a larger area. On the other hand, when a person is sick or fearful and tense, they contract to about half their size, and then their color changes from a transparent blue to a pale color of a yellowish shade. Just as with the auras, successful bioenergetic treatment causes the chakras to change colors so that they are clearer, shine more brightly, and are more vital, and they then radiate a great deal of vitality.

It is important to cleanse a person's chakras because they absorb traumas, tensions, and waste energy. When I treat a person bioenergetically, I draw out, with my hands, the waste energy accumulated in the chakras. After they are emptied, they are filled with better vital energy which I cause to flow into them. The purpose of the treatment is thus to permit the flow of better energy into the body. The chakras "nourish" the organs with energy as they transfer impulses and waves to every affected molecule of the body.

Charging the chakras with energy varies from one person to another; there are some who will retain the charge for a long period of time, even up to a year, while with others the energy charges to the chakras dissipate in a matter of days or even hours. People who are healthy and relatively calm recharge themselves, and thus these energies are retained for a long time. However, illness, emotional tensions, fear, and skepticism cause the energy to be dissipated more rapidly. There is a very fast dissipation of energy among those suffering from cancer, for instance. Physical labor does not cause a loss of energy; it is one's emotional state that brings it about. The ideal patient is the one who easily and swiftly absorbs the energies and then preserves them in his body for an extended period of time. Our body attracts as much energy as it needs. When I no longer feel the vibrations in my hands during the course of the treatment, it is a sign to me that I should terminate the treatment.

The meridians are transportation channels which carry the energy, passing through the head at the crown chakra and then flowing to the different parts of the body; they look like fluorescent strands. I see the meridians in groups of five, as sheaves of shining light which connect the chakra of the crown to that of the third eye, then to that of the heart where the groups of five split up to the hands and feet; and there, again, there are groups of five meridians for each hand and foot. In the upper part of the body, the division begins at the chakra of the throat, and in the lower part it is at the chakra of the base.

Sometimes the meridians appear to me like a stream of shiny water as it emerges from a syringe, the "fountain" being the chakra of the crown. The meridians and the chakras are bound together, and a blockage or injury to either can be the source of an injury or disease in one of the organs of the body.

I am able to identify meridians at problematic areas that indicate an energy blockage. For example, with some patients I am able to see on a group of meridians, which look like strings, a bluish stain from which something akin to a stress of energy flows to the injured organ. This is due to the effort by the meridian to transfer energy to the injured or diseased area, and it is possible that a blockage was created in the transfer of beneficial energy to the injured area. When that organ receives healing energy, the relief is felt not only in the organ itself but is visible in that the bluish color of the meridians dissolves and disappears. During the course of the bioenergetic treatment, the meridians are another tool for me to draw the waste energy out of the body.

I divide my bioenergetic treatment into three stages: In the first stage, I pass my hands over the entire body and over the energy hubs using my palms, causing energies to flow into them and fill them, and then, as I pass over the meridians, transferring energy to them and "moving" it to all parts of the body. In the second stage, I draw the waste energy out through the chakras and meridians. The vital energy continues to circulate in the body, while the waste exits through the meridians at the feet or through the chakra of the crown at the head. In the third stage, I pass my hands over the affected organ itself and over the bluish stain on the meridians. As I see it, my work is based on the assumption that first and foremost I have to fill the chakra hubs with energy so that there will not be any vacuum after the removal of the waste energy. The object is to prevent the loss of energy which is meant to reach the diseased region, for if there is a vacuum present, it will draw the beneficial energy away from where it is needed. Only afterwards do I draw the waste out and concentrate on the area of the injured part of the body.

I can never predict how the bioenergetic treatment will affect an individual patient. For example, two sisters came to me for bioenergetic treatment. One of them felt strong sensations during the treatment and claimed she felt much better, whereas the other sister felt nothing. There were also marked differences in the reaction of the meridians; one sister was able to absorb more energy than the other. I cannot predict how many treatments a person will need or how many treatments it will take for the opening and release of blockages in the chakras and meridians. A course of treatment generally varies between a single visit to twelve visits. Many times patients do not return. Only later do I find out the reason for this. Sometimes it is because they felt much better; in other cases, they felt that I did not help them; alternately, they felt no change after the first session and decided not to return. On average, I have between four and six sessions with a patient. When I feel that my ability to help a person is limited, I terminate the treatment.

Even though I serve as a conduit for the flow of energy and am automatically recharged, I have developed a number of exercises to fill myself with added energy. In the early morning hours, I walk out to the sand dunes at the outskirts of the city near my home and proceed to my regular place under an ancient sycamore tree, a relic of the time before the blight of city concrete infringed on nature. This particular sycamore tree is ancient, and I found it when I felt the tremendous energy emanating from it on one of my walks years ago. When I sat down underneath it at that time, I felt a great spiritual power. I sit between its exposed roots, the yellowish sand "flowing" around me silently, my back resting on the broad trunk, its branches offering welcome shade and refreshing the soul. Within a few minutes I enter into meditation, and the silence all about me enables me to concentrate better. Sometimes, a mantra helps me in my meditational concentration and enables me to enter more deeply into myself.

After about twenty minutes, I return to the sensory world, apart from the peaceful meditational dimension, and I remain at peace, my back still resting on the gnarled trunk with its deep fissures. Now I begin breathing exercises. I breathe deeply the fresh air and hold the air within me. When I inhale, in my mind I move the oxygen and energy to various parts of my body by concentrating on the part of my body where I wish to send the oxygen. During this process, I blow the air and filter it out of my mouth while making a soft sound, slowly, over a long period of time. During the process of absorbing energies into my body, I begin (in my mind) at my feet, transferring energy to them, continuing on to the chest, the hands, the head, each time breathing a few times and transferring the energies to all of my body. Throughout the length of my body, I feel the flow of the energy. Afterwards, I sit with my body limp and the palms of my hands open. I feel the energy flowing to every part of my body, the current itching my palms. At the end of this process, I stand up slowly.

As he applied his gift of healing people, Ze'ev, a man with an insatiable curiosity, wondered what it was he did that worked. He became familiar with the aura—the electromagnetic field that is the seat of our life force and personality—that extends slightly beyond our skin. Thus, bioenergetic treatments are most of all just above the surface of the body where they affect the outer limit of the aura, the very center of the "problem" the healer tries to cure. Ze'ev now knew that his gift was not in contravention of natural law, not a suspension of what we presently know of physics and physiology, but rather was a new and powerful tool.

7

Visions and Visualizations: The Gift Expands

While Ze'ev was seeing more and more patients, a curious thing happened: He began to see not only the discoloration of people's auras, indicating illness or damage, but also parts of their problems, experiences, and, in some cases, existence of previous lives somehow connected to the suffering they were experiencing in this life. Obtaining this more detailed information enabled Ze'ev to concentrate more fully on their problems.

This is not so surprising; the more we use the powers of extrasensory perception—the psychic ability—the more it grows. Contrary to all other forms of expended energy, which diminish when we use them, psychic and with it bioenergetic energy increases in direct proportion to its usage! It would appear to me, therefore, that the traumatic incident in the Sinai, with its enveloping white cloud, had initiated a process of paranormal energy growth which was now following that law. The more Ze'ev used it, the more it grew.

When a person sits opposite me, I examine the electro-magnetic field which surrounds him, his aura and the shafts of light emanating from him. Sometimes, in these shafts of light, pictures appear. Beyond the first aura closest to the person there is the second aura, composed of various layers and shades. Sometimes pictures appear there that relate to other periods in the life of the person. It is in this section of the aura that I sometimes see previous incarnations.

Beyond the second section, at the highest part of the human aura, there sometimes appear the figures of relatives or spirit guides. The pictures appear like a panoramic film that can be seen over a large area with perspective and depth, shadows that look like negatives, sometimes including very real-looking figures. In some cases I can see the various periods of the person's life in a structure, similar to a long tunnel, at the end of which there is a point of light. That light appears in different colors, sometimes bean-shaped or elliptical; it shines brightly enough to blind one. But I cannot see what occurs beyond it. The light point appears either about eight inches above the person's head or very high on the ceiling or against the walls of the room. I have no idea when and why the light point will appear in certain instances and not in others.

Sometime in 1984, I set up an appointment for a patient; she was the last one that night. It was a winter evening, cold and damp. The patient just before her left the treatment room, and while I escorted him to the door I saw the next patient sitting in the waiting room. I sat down opposite her, looking at her. I asked her why she had come, and she informed me that she suffered from locked knees, meaning that for years she had been unable to walk the way everyone else does, but that her legs dragged her as if they were two firm rods, without flexibility and the ability to bend, even though she was able to sit with her knees bent. As she spoke I focused my gaze on her aura and entered into a deep trance, and suddenly I saw pictures of her life. "I see you at about five or six years of age, living in Jaffa; the house has three stories, a very old house. I see you running and skipping on the steps from the top floor to the ground. You are running down the stairs, and on the landing between the second and first floors, I see you stepping on a bird. You are stepping on a bird."

Then, in the middle of the sentence, the woman became hysterical, crying and shouting, "I know why I walk this way! God punished me, because I stepped on the bird . . . God punished me . . . because I stepped on the bird." Her crying tore at my heart. The room filled with fog, and its color turned white from the force of the energy present in it. I went over to her, placed my hands on her knees, and transmitted energy to her legs, my movements pulling downward and then upward toward her waist, back and forth. I then commanded her to get up and walk. She listened and spontaneously stood up, tears still in her eyes, and began walking about carefully, pacing slowly about the room, bending her knees, and walking normally.

In the first year I worked at the clinic near my home in Holon, in 1982, a woman from Ramat Gan called and asked to make an appointment for a woman who lived on the island of Malta who was due to arrive in Israel in a fortnight. Gloria turned out to be an attractive woman in her fifties. I still had to complete the treatment of the patient before her, and she sat down in an armchair and awaited her turn. When she entered the treatment room, I studied her aura even before she had had a chance to tell me anything and concentrated with all my might as the words slowly started flowing from my mouth. "I see you in Manchester, in a two-story wooden home, with a husband and a daughter, a little girl. It is cold outside, a night in February, and you are in the house. I hear a sudden explosion from the direction of the back of the building, and I see you upstairs; the house goes up in flames. You run to the baby's room to save her. You manage to get the child out of the bed amidst the confusion. I see you running down the burning stairs with the baby. You manage to save her from the burning building. You cry out, 'Save my husband! My husband is inside the house!' The firemen try to save him, but I see him remaining in the burning house, burning to death." I finished what I had to say as if from a deep sleep and looked at her face. From her left eye fell a solitary tear. She remained mute as a result of the great shock at what she had heard.

She confirmed what I had said was true. She then went on to tell me that after her husband's death she had taken her daughter and returned to her parents' home in Tel Aviv. One day she met a certain wealthy man from the island of Malta, the two becoming very close, eventually marrying. The couple, together with her daughter, moved to Malta.

While she was still telling me this, her face became distorted suddenly, her hands began to tremble, and her head began to roll from side to side involuntarily; her throat emitted screeching sounds. Her hands and feet flew up and down with twisted, rapid movements. Her eyes rolled in their sockets. I wasn't sure whether I should summon help. Instead, I began to treat her. I do not know from where I drew the powers to continue to deal with her without letup, passing my hands over her, transmitting energy to her. I stood next to her for close to an hour and treated her until her body finally calmed down, became quiet, and the movements ceased. I was exhausted, my powers drained. We did, however, make an appointment for another treatment a few days later.

The time came and the doorbell rang. This time Gloria arrived with a big yellow sunflower in her hand. This unusual gesture was very pleasant, and I expressed my thanks. As she entered the room, she again and again thanked me for the treatment she had received and declared her amazement at the results. Since then the number of attacks had begun to diminish, and both the force and the frequency of the attacks had decreased.

I concentrated deeply a second time on her electromagnetic field. As I concentrated I suddenly saw the entity of a woman standing behind her, a dark figure with hair long and black framing an elongated face with protruding cheekbones, wearing a dress reminding me of a gypsy. I concentrated even harder, and on the figure's hand I clearly saw a bracelet. I turned to the patient, describing the figure of the woman I saw within the white fog in which she had appeared. "Yes, I know who it is," Gloria stated, "the gypsy that comes to our home from time to time! She tells the future in coffee cups; the bracelet you described she gave me as a gift."

I told her to dispose of the bracelet as soon as she returned to Malta, to throw it into a river or burn it so that it would not get into any other person's hands and transfer to him the negative magic embedded in it.

Gloria returned to her home in Malta, and two months passed until she contacted me again. "The moment I arrived home, I opened the drawer and the bracelet was not in the place I had left it. I searched for it feverishly, and in the end I found it, to my astonishment, within a boot in the shoe closet, and to this day I do not know how it got there. I pulled it out of the boot, wrapped it in a piece of fabric, and my husband and I drove to the other side of the river. The bracelet fell into the river and was submerged in the water. I feel fantastic, the attacks have disappeared, as if they had never existed, and I have never seen the gypsy since then. She disappeared, as if she had never existed."

Here we have a classic example of how a psychic healer can at times extend the gift to prophecy and clairvoyance. The woman from Malta had a terrible affliction for which there would have been no rational explanation, if it were not for Ze'ev's vision about her. Only then did the treatment he gave her afterwards make sense and lead to an understanding of what had caused the afflic-tion in the first place.

Could a "gypsy curse" really cause such things? Gypsies are often maligned, and frequently without good cause. But here we have an attractive woman with a big house and a wealthy husband, and a hardworking fortune teller, perhaps filled with envy. She expresses her frustration by wishing her patron evil—leading her to believe the gift was a friend's offering, when in fact it was merely a contact by which the link between them was strengthened.

Did the gypsy program the bracelet to cause the woman dis-tress? Perhaps, and thoughts are powerful energies, especially when negatively accented.

Breaking the contact by disposing of the bracelet had two dif-ferent results: physically, it removed the link-object from the person of the woman, thus breaking the hold of the affliction that went with it; psychologically, the act of throwing the offending bracelet into the river cleansed the woman from the evil it had brought her, assuring her unconscious that she was now safe from its influences.

In 1985 there arrived at my clinic a young Druze woman, aged twenty, accompanied by her family. They came from a Druze village in the Galilee mountains; this young woman, Suham, had just been married, her husband being one of the group. As the family observed its religious tenets scrupulously and had to protect the young woman's modesty, her father and brother entered my treatment room with her while her young husband remained in the waiting room with the rest of the fam-ily. The Druze people have a firm belief in reincarnation and life after death. They do not bury people individually, but rather in large common graves, as they claim the body has no real value and the soul will in any event live again in the body of someone else of their community.

The couple had had a lavish wedding, but the morning after the wedding, when Suham awoke, she arose from the bed and, to her husband's horror, acted like a woman with an entirely different personality and behavior pattern from the one he knew. The family panicked. They sought help and decided to come to me for advice.

Suham entered the room with her face the epitome of panic, her eyes large and wide open. She gazed into the air. She sat down opposite me and began reaching out for the different items on my desk, touching and feeling them; her body was restless and fidgety, her hands not stopping for an instant as she kept moving items around, changing their order over and over. "What is your name?" I asked her, and she answered, "Nadia." Her brother shook his head vigorously and immediately said, "No. She is not Nadia. That is the name that she constantly claims is hers, and when she uses that name she acts like an entirely different woman, not the one that we know, our daughter and sister, Suham." Indeed, all of Nadia's behavior was spontaneous and casual, something unacceptable among the women of the Druze. I tried to speak to her again, but she began to sing and refused to speak. After a few minutes, suddenly the woman's face was changed, her eyes contracted, and now it was a helpless look, one which elicited pity. She became quiet, well-mannered, somewhat withdrawn, sitting on the chair obediently. Again, I asked for her name. She answered with sorrow in her eyes, "Suham." "How do you feel, Suham?" I continued. She answered, "Not good, I feel very bad. I am tired . . . very tired." I looked into her aura and was astounded to see clearly in the reflection a shadow of another entity. A short time later there again was a marked change in the young woman, and Nadia appeared once more, a liberated woman, her behavior radiating confidence. Once again I asked for her name. "Nadia," she answered. "What is the name of your father?" "Fadac." "The name of your mother?" "Raida." "Where were you Nadia, before you entered Suham's body?" "I lived in Akalon, in the village of Akalon in Lebanon," she answered. "Why did you enter Suham?" "Because she is pretty," she answered me. "How did you get to her?" She answered, "I was at her wedding. I danced with her the entire evening of the wedding." "How did you enter her body?" "When her husband penetrated her, I entered her through the hymen."

Suham's father and brother sat as if turned to stone, listening to what was happening. "At what age did you die, Nadia?" "When I was twenty-eight," she responded. "How? Why did you die?" There was a short silence, and Nadia answered, "My grandfather killed me with an ax blow to my throat." "Why?" "I became friendly with intellectuals in Lebanon, and grandfather suspected that I had overstepped the bounds of modesty and killed me because he felt that I had defiled the honor of the family. He told me that he wanted to speak to me, and asked that I accompany him. We went down the hill to a hut that leads to the fields. Suddenly, he took out an ax and killed me." Nadia then took a pen and a pad that had been lying on my desk and began to draw pictures of figures, and noted next to every organ and part of the body their names and explanations. I asked her, "What was your occupation?" "I was an author and poet," she answered, then took the pen and pad and with a clenched fist began automatically to write down her thoughts in Arabic. Then her hand fell down and became weak. I said, "I am asking you to leave Suham's body, Nadia." But Nadia refused. "I will not leave Suham!" I continued, adamantly, "You have to leave her!" She suddenly cried out in a loud voice, took off her kerchief, twisted about on the chair, and screamed, "I will not leave! . . . I will not leave! . . . I don't want to leave!" As she screamed she again grabbed the pen forcibly and scribbled with great vigor, as if erasing and annulling everything she had written earlier. She began to breathe in and out very deeply. As she made sounds of exhaling the air in her, she sighed and groaned and again became Suham, and this went back and forth several times.

I asked for guidance, and suddenly I felt a tremendous force in my body, and when Nadia was again opposite me I told her in an authoritative voice, "Leave the body of the woman Suham." She did not respond. Again I commanded her, "Nadia, you have to leave Suham's body." Then, finally a sound of sobbing emanated from her throat, like the wailing of the wind, like a strange lamentation. Nadia continued sobbing like this for a number of minutes. Again I turned to her and said, "Nadia, leave her body; you are disturbing her ability to live." She answered, "We don't want to leave . . . we want to remain!

We don't want to leave! . . . We won't go!" I repeated, "Leave Suham's body . . ." This time she answered in the singular, "No! . . . No! . . . I won't leave!"

This difficult dialogue continued for about two hours. I ordered and Nadia refused. But slowly, her voice began to get weaker and her head began to sway to the side. "I am tired . . . I am very tired. . . ." she said. "In the name of all the saints that you believe in," I said, "leave Suham's body." As her weariness increased, she again began to mumble. Suddenly, I heard a strong sound of wings behind my back. I turned around and saw that two pure white doves had landed on the windowsill. In seconds it occurred to me that they were carrying a message with them. The father and brother were overcome at the sight. The doves remained on the windowsill for a number of minutes, flapped their wings, and then flew away. The body of the young woman opposite me seemed to flutter, too, and gradually she began to calm down and eventually came to herself, very weary, drained from the effort and not remembering or knowing anything that had happened. I then treated her and built up the defensive energy field around her body.

I, too, was drained and tired. Suham returned to her previous state and returned with her family to their home in the hills of Galilee.

My role in this event was more that of a medium, a role which connected Suham and Nadia—a type of mediator. I have no doubt that Nadia's surrender was brought about by the power of my spiritual guides. In the dialogue I conducted, I was directed by spiritual guidance, saying what I did without knowing or being aware of any guidelines that came from my own awareness.

Did Ze'ev go beyond the work of a bioenergetic healer in this case? He certainly did, but then mediumship (which healing also is) has many facets, and sometimes more than one phase comes into play, if the case requires it. This case certainly fit that category. Ze'ev approached the question of possession from a spiritual angle, which is in keeping with his particular abilities. He is not a parapsychologist, and perhaps a trained and experienced investigator would have demanded more detailed evidence from the woman to truly prove the account. Just the same, Ze'ev succeeded admirably and then applied his bioenergetic approach to close the case.

Ze'ev remembers another client:

A man looking about thirty-two came to me with a complaint of strong pains in the neck, after having gone to various doctors for the previous two years. All the tests showed no physiological explanation for his pains. The pain in his neck was so intense that it affected him even at night when his head was resting on a pillow. He was a driver by profession. I looked at his aura, and the colors were very dark, a metallic blue and yellow. Within his energy field I saw a clear picture which I assumed was from a previous incarnation. The year was 1906—that was the number which appeared before my eyes. I suddenly saw the man sitting across from me in a little village I just knew to be in southern France. People were dragging him out of his house and hanging him from a tree. His neck was broken, and I suddenly realized that this was the source of the pain that had remained from his previous incarnation. He looked about thirty, and when the pains appeared in this incarnation, two years earlier, the man was also about thirty. In the picture, the hanging was extremely gruesome, as was the way his face appeared twisted. I then proceeded to treat this man. The energy field around his neck was dust-colored, and I removed the shell of the energy field from this region of his body. The pains disappeared as a result of the treatment, as if they had never existed.

Ze'ev is not alone in trying to ferret out problems from previous lives and bringing them to the surface, thereby resolving them for the sufferer. The result is that an illness caused by a problem from a previous lifetime, which otherwise would not be understood, is no longer able to cause symptoms in this life. Conventional medical treatment or psychiatric evaluation would totally miss the real cause of the problem and would not be able to resolve it.

Dr. William Yaney of Beverly Hills, California, is a pioneer in treating patients by referring to their previous lives as a source for the required treatment in this lifetime. He is not a paranormal healer but a renowned medical doctor and psychiatrist, and he is not alone in the approach. Increasing numbers of doctors take quite seriously symptoms caused by situations in previous lives that are unknown to the sufferer, because there are positive results to back them up. When the patient understands the origin of the affliction, it appears that the matter is solved with or without the use of deep hypnotic regression, though preferably with the latter.

8

Absent Healing:
Healing from a Distance—
Does It Work?

It is no secret that in psychic matters, distance—and frequently time—as we understand the terms, are of no importance. If all psychic phenomena, including healing, take place in a dimension not subject to the usual limitations of time and space (and evidence strongly suggests that), then it should also be possible for Ze'ev to "send" his bioenergies to a patient not in his physical presence.

I should emphasize here that we are not talking about religious or quasi-religious "tuning-in" sessions of large groups of people to derive certain benefits. These benefits, in my view, are more philosophical and spiritual than specific and tangible in the usual sense, spontaneous healing at faith-healing sessions notwithstanding. When they do occur (and are truly genuine, not hysterical or pretended), they are mostly due to the patient's own awakened powers of self-healing, triggered by a powerful orator or minister and supported by a strong desire to be healed. Wonderful, if and when it has genuine results.

What Ze'ev does when he undertakes healing over distances is not an emotional appeal or a quasi-religious service. Instead, he sends his healing energies to the patient. It is perhaps a moot point whether he sends energies to the patient through a telepathic process or whether he manages to project himself, or a part of himself, and perform the healing at a distance as himself. If the results are evidential, so much the better. Results are usually better when the patient has had an initial visit, later followed up with distant sessions over the telephone.

But let Ze'ev speak for himself:

In October of 1988 a woman named Pesiah telephoned me from New York, having heard about me from friends. For four months she had been confined to bed because of severe back problems, and there was no relief or cure in sight. Pesiah offered to send me an airline ticket to New York so that I could come and treat her. But I could not fulfill her request; my appointment book showed lists of many patients waiting for aid, and in spite of her distress I never considered such a trip. I thought for a second and asked Pesiah to lie down in bed and to hold the telephone in her hand. I concentrated, and with my spiritual eye I saw a picture of Pesiah. I had never met the woman before, but I was still able to see a picture of her. I concentrated on her spine and began to transmit energy to her through the center of my third eye, not unlike a laser beam, using my mind to transmit energy to her whole body. I held the telephone in Israel, and she held the telephone in New York. I concentrated primarily on the pelvic region, where I felt that her problem was. About five minutes later, Pesiah said that her whole body was burning and especially the lower back in the area of the pelvis. I then commanded, "Get up from your bed and tell me how you feel." Pesiah got up from her bed and cried with joy, "I'm walking! . . . I'm standing on my legs!" Indeed, Pesiah walked now as if nothing had ever happened to her.

Two months later I did indeed travel to the United States, and while there visited with Pesiah. I recognized her immediately.

One can compare our thoughts to radio waves, which can be sent and transmitted beyond one's physical place and received at the other end provided that there is a receiver tuned to the right wavelength. I am able to transmit energy through the force of my thoughts, and the person at the other end absorbs the energy and "opens" his channels to the proper wavelength.

At the time when I worked in a medical clinic in Netanya, a patient I knew arrived together with her friend from Ireland, named Jill. She was about thirty years old, a dancer by trade, short of stature, very thin, and with a fragile appearance. She was suffering from a general, inexplicable weakness that made movement of the body difficult. Jill was especially concerned, being a dancer. My treatments helped her greatly, and she felt now in excellent health and returned to Ireland, but we agreed that during the following summer I would transmit energy to her from afar. A number of months went by and Jill's friend came to the clinic, bearing a letter addressed to me. Even before she handed me the letter, I heard myself say, "You know, in August I concentrated on Jill and transmitted energy to her, as we had spoken of my sending her energy from afar. I am happy to receive a letter from her, but as I do not read English well, could you please read the letter to me." In her letter Jill wrote, "I feel marvelous, and indeed, on the 15th of August I felt energy from you throughout my body. It was a feeling similar to the energy I received from you at the clinic in Israel; I knew it was coming from you."

In November of 1988, just before I traveled to the United States, Shmulik Rochenberger, a friend who had just arrived from the United States, called and asked for my help. In a trembling voice he told me that his father had had a stroke and was now hospitalized in very critical condition in the hospital in Kfar Sava. Shmulik asked me to transmit energy to his father from where I was while I was still treating people in the clinic. There were still patients awaiting their turn, so we agreed that when I completed my work at exactly 10:30 P.M. I would rest for awhile and at 11:00 I would enter a state of deep concentration in order to transmit healing energy to his father. We also agreed between us that Shmulik would stand near his father's bed with his hands spread over him, exactly at the time we had decided upon, and I would transmit energy *through him.*

I also asked Shmulik for details of the exact place where his father was hospitalized. I remember that it was in the Department of Internal Medicine in the hospital, on the fifth floor. Close to about 10:30 I finished my work for the day, drained and tired. Nevertheless, I felt a tremendous desire to help Shmulik's father, and at that moment I decided to drive to the hospital, a distance of about twenty miles. Something inside me told me to drive even though it was already well into the night and in spite of my exhaustion and my imminent departure for the United States the next day. I did not call Shmulik, nor did I tell him that I was on my way.

The throughway spread before me; the headlights of cars in the other lane whizzed by me; the night was cool. The entire way I paid attention to the clock, remembering that we had decided upon exactly 11:00 P.M. As I was afraid I might be late, I began to concentrate and beam energy to Shmulik while I was still in the car. I finally arrived. The hospital gates are generally closed by that time, but for some reason they were wide open and there was no guard at the gate. I entered and ran up toward the room in which Shmulik's father lay. The patients' rooms were already dark, and the time by my watch was exactly 11:00 P.M. By the dim light of the room, I saw Shmulik standing next to his father's bed with his hands above the bed; his entire energy field shone with a violet color. At that moment I knew that I had succeeded in transferring healing energy through Shmulik—the beginning of the aid to his father—by transmitting energy from a distance.

Now I was at Shmulik's side and transferred energy to his father; a few minutes later the patient began breathing normally. By the end of my visit we were even able to speak a few words with the father. The next day Shmulik called me and told me that his father had gotten up from his bed that morning, had stood up, and afterwards sat in a wheelchair. A week later, his father was already moving around with a walker.

In this case, my aim was to transmit healing energy to another person (Shmulik) so that he would do the healing, having him act as a conduit for healing, as I myself was unable to physically heal the patient at the time. Shmulik's violet halo was charged with healing energy during those times after I had transmitted it to him from my car. Shmulik's father's condition had been deteriorating consistently for some time and the height of the crisis had been reached the night I came to treat him. From that point on, there was dramatic improvement in his father's condition.

Absent healing is not unique with Ze'ev, though his dramatic results are quite outstanding and remind me of the impact Cayce had on those who sought his help. In ancient times, Ze'ev would have been considered a saint or a supernatural being to be venerated or a witch to be persecuted, depending on the state of the culture in which such events may have occurred. In our time, the wider scientific community is just beginning to awaken to the enormous potential rare individuals like Ze'ev offer in exploring alternative areas of medicine and healing; but so much prejudice and ignorance of what we are is yet to be overcome. Modern science is an unfinished building in need of several more floors and a roof! The use of a surrogate to transfer energy and to act under his control is, in my estimation, unique with Ze'ev. I am glad it works.

PART TWO

9

The Successful Healer

M any great talents, especially in the arts, have to go abroad to be recognized and later appreciated at home. Not so with Ze'ev. As soon as he had set up his clinic in Israel, not far from his home, word got around that he was a man who could help people who had not been helped by doctors and conventional medicine. This was not some mystical guru who required allegiance to his particular brand of faith for a healing to occur. Far from it. Ze'ev had not changed one bit from the simple, practical, and curious person he had always been long before he became a healer. He neither advertised nor sought patients. The media in his country heard of cases that had been cured, and gradually their interviews—sometimes straight and proper, sometimes more sensational and sloppy—spread the word to those who could read Hebrew.

Curiously, or perhaps not so for a man also deeply interested in the mystic, Ze'ev is totally convinced of the laws of karma and the reality of reincarnation. But he also applies these convictions to his work: those who are meant to be helped will be, if their destinies permit it. To some, this may sound like a cop-out, but Ze'ev means it deeply and passionately. Without being partisan to any sect or religious faction, and nominally Jewish, Ze'ev always looks beyond the human hierarchy of any organized faith directly to the Godhead for guidance, inspiration, and help with his work. And he makes a particular point of how important a patient's attitude toward the spiritual, especially spiritual healing, may influence the outcome.

Diseases—physical or mental infirmities—are part of the tribulations a person is confronted with during his life. However, healing or the amount of suffering (until one is healed) are determined by one's karma and are linked to providence, in my view. Many times when I help patients, I am being asked, "Why didn't we get to you earlier?" The explanation for this, I tell them, is that whatever happens to us in our lives does so at its proper time. Nothing happens by chance. The primary condition for a person to be healed through bioenergy is his readiness at the time he comes to me to receive healing energy, to the extent the patient has sufficient openness and faith to absorb whatever I can give and transfer to him. I have met people who disapproved of me and demanded that I prove my ability. These people's blockage is extremely strong, and rather than utilizing their desire to be healed and to cooperate, most of their power is expended in resisting. With such people, there is very little I can do.

The same happens when a patient comes to me against his will due to family pressures. I remember a case where an exceptionally ill woman came to my clinic after her family had begged her and put pressure on her to try it. A few minutes after I began to treat her, she suddenly turned to me in agitation and asked, "Well, when will you be finished?" I tried to placate her and to ask her to be patient, but she continued and answered impatiently that her time was limited and that she had to hurry and finish doing her shopping in the market. Even though the family believed in the treatment, the patient's intellectual opposition was so strong that it blocked off her channels from absorbing energy. I saw no reason to continue the treatment and stopped it.

Thought and will power are mighty forces that enable us to open the energy hubs of the body. I believe that with correct thought, a person can heal himself, too. When a patient by the power of his thought opposes bioenergetic treatment, it leads to blockage of the energy fields and their hubs in his body. When there is resistance, the aura appears asymmetric, with an ash-metallic color, or I see in it bumps, which I attribute to blockage. In such situations, I try to heal the person during a session or two, and if there is no improvement I give up.

If the physical problem is of karmic origin, the aid that spiritual healing can offer will only be partial or temporary, and, as I understand it, the person must change those factors in his behavior that brought about this karma. Indeed, it is important to understand that bioenergetic treatment is linked to the spiritual world and to reasons of providence which brought about the illness or will bring about the cure. As the Jewish sages put it, "Everything is foreseen, yet one has the right to act" (as he wishes). It is true that suffering is decreed as a person's lot, but for us to be cured we have to look deeply into ourselves and understand that a complete cure will come only when it is in keeping with our deeds and behavior.

On occasion, I have refused requests for treatment by people who were ill, based on the description of their illness, for I was convinced I could not help them. Yet, after having been pressured by them, I finally agreed to accept them, and in the end the treatment helped them significantly. There are times when I look at a patient I have treated and feel a sense of awe at the merciful healing that takes place with my assistance. Such divine beauty may be found, I feel, in the story of the healing of Ido Angel, a boy of 11½, whom I met and treated when he was ill. One evening at the clinic, the telephone rang. I was informed that the son of Aviva Angel, whom I already knew for some time, was very sick and had been hospitalized in the children's department of the Tel Hashomer Hospital. The doctors believed that he had but a few hours to live. It was asked that I make an effort to come to the hospital and help the child. I had finished a full day's work at about 9:00 P.M. and was utterly exhausted. What I wanted most right then was to come home, shower, and regain my strength by resting. I nevertheless found it difficult to refuse a request for help, and entered my car and drove to the hospital.

The lobby leading to the children's department was packed from wall to wall with people who had come to be with their children. In one of the corners sat Ido's parents. When they saw me, they greeted me warmly while expressing their astonishment that I had even come. Ido had an extremely high temperature of 106 degrees that had not come down for a month, and there was no way to help him. Ido's condition was terminal. We proceeded to the room where their son lay. In a bed near the window, I saw Ido lying unmoving and hooked up intravenously, and it appeared to me that he was unconscious. I stood opposite Ido's bed, observing the intravenous tubes entering him and the other medical equipment to which he was attached. I then concentrated on him with all my might. As I did so, I suddenly detached myself from everything about me and focused my vision deeply into the energy fields around his body. I saw that his aura shone in an asymmetric manner and that the energy around him was not uniform. In my heart I asked for the help of my spiritual guides in the treatment process, and while I still whispered my prayer, I walked over slowly and began to radiate energy to his body, from his head to his toes and back, continuing for a number of minutes until I felt that his body was beginning to cool down as I passed my hands over him. With my eyes closed, I felt how the room had become filled with the strong energy of healing.

Ido began to sweat profusely, and the robe that he was wearing was covered in a matter of minutes with large sweat stains while his forehead and face were bathed in sweat. I continued to draw out more and more waste energy from his body, feeling the negative energy in the palms of my hands. Suddenly, there was the sharp sound of an explosion, like a short circuit, and when I heard the sound I felt that I had finished, for the time being. The palms of my hands were heavy and hot, itching terribly, as a result of the waste energy I had drawn out. I turned to the sink on the northern wall of the room to wash my hands after completing the treatment. Suddenly, I heard the voice of a child. I turned around and saw that Ido was sitting up on his bed, with his hands stretched out, looking in amazement and confusion, and asking, "What am I doing here?" Aviva ran over to her son, hugged him, and kissed him. She then explained to him why he was there. Ido calmed down after hearing her explanation, clearly exhausted, and then fell asleep, his breathing becoming normal.

It appears that for some time Ido had been suffering from terrible stomach pains. The family doctor had claimed that it must be some type of virus. But Ido's condition grew progressively worse and the pain became unbearable. The child was therefore brought to the hospital, where intensive tests were begun to diagnose the problem. The tests went on for about three weeks without treatment, and the doctors were inclined to think that the child was suffering from a rare condition which was incurable. The child became as thin as a skeleton, bent over both physically and emotionally. One day the doctors gave up completely. They summoned the parents and told them that they saw no great hope for his life.

After further treatment I told Aviva that the night might be difficult because there would be a reaction from the treatment, but I promised that by the next morning Ido would be completely back to normal. The night turned into a nightmare; Ido sweated the whole night through and cried out in pain as the disease was beginning to leave his body. The following morning, at five o'clock, the doctor came in, looked at Ido, and said, "What a miracle!"

After I had successfully treated Ido, the mother of the girl in the next bed asked me to help her twelve-year-old daughter, who was unable to fall soundly asleep and who had suffered from this for years without any relief. After a short treatment in which I transferred energy to her, the girl indeed fell asleep. I then went from bed to bed radiating energy to all the children in the room. At the end I stopped next to the bed of a child who lay alone without any relatives, and I felt a strong desire to help him, even if he would never know about it, because there was no adult there to ask treatment for him. A few days later, Aviva told me excitedly that all the children who had been in the ward that night had been released from the hospital within a short period of time!

That Ze'ev could enter public and private hospitals without interference from the medical establishment, at least in Israel, speaks for their attitude toward any help they can get. It is not so easy in the United States, where powerful medical and pharmaceutical lobbies are jealously guarding their precincts, even to the detriment of their patients' potential healing. Still, the doors are beginning to open a little here, too, as indeed they have long been in other, less "sophisticated" countries like Brazil and England (by sophisticated I mean the unwillingness to consider alternative paths to anything, especially good health).

As for the dying boy, Ido, an infection of unknown origin was his problem. Because all known remedies to defeat that infection, that toxic energy, as Ze'ev would call it, had failed, we can see that Ze'ev possessed an energy superior to those remedies, as indeed he does. If a damaged energy field, or aura, is at the base of illness (and I think it is), then powerful positively charged energy, bio-energy in this case, can "burn out" the damaged parts of the energy field and replace it with fresh, healthy energy—thus making the patient well again. There is nothing startlingly new about this concept. Cayce had the same explanation. The only difference is, Ze'ev has this power in large doses, thanks to the incident in the Sinai.

10

Common Ailments Yielding to Kolman's Treatments

Some doctors coming to my clinic to ask for bioenergetic treatment often wish to remain anonymous, not because they do not believe in the treatment, but because openness to alternative medicine is still in its infancy. Bioenergy is not meant to replace conventional medicine, but to work alongside medicine and to offer assistance to it. I cannot serve as a substitute for a doctor, and when a patient arrives with severe physical problems, I make sure he has first sought the assistance of conventional medicine. If he tells me that medicine cannot offer a solution for him, I offer my assistance. Sometimes I am asked by patients whether they should decrease or stop the medication they have been prescribed, and my answer always is that the prescribing doctor is the only authority for this. It is for him to examine the patient after a number of bioenergetic treatments, he being the sole authority as to what extent to change the existing treatment. Some doctors send me patients after they are unable to do anything more for them. Bioenergy can hasten the healing in places which have been injured, such as in knitting together sections cut apart as part of an operation or binding bones after fractures. It helps in chronic conditions, such as repeated infections, inexplicable pain, or allergies. Bioenergy cannot under any circumstances harm anyone.

In his work at the clinic, it soon became clear to Ze'ev which illnesses he was able to cure more often than others. He knows perfectly well that he is not God and cannot heal everyone, but there were enough cases of successful healing to show that he was able to deal with illness effectively many times, often when conventional medicine could not. He kept a careful log of his treatments and the results. It soon became clear that certain kinds of problems were brought to him more often than others and again that he was usually able to deal with them successfully.

Despite his evident successes, Ze'ev still had no real idea how the healing worked, even though he understood by now the functions of chakras and bioenergetic energy, his great gift. Somewhat childlike, nevertheless, he remained in awe of his accomplishments, forever surprised when something particularly exciting became a fact in the course of his ministrations. One need only compare this attitude to that of the faith healers in the United States and their often spurious claims, their financial greed, and their pseudo-religious fervor (not to mention their lack of results) to appreciate Ze'ev's personal position in respect to his powers.

Although he has been willing to try helping anyone and any kind of ailment (unless an inner voice might tell him he should not, for some reason), some of the more common problems, according to Ze'ev, are these.

Back Pain

Back pain is common. It is often caused by an incorrect posture, by carrying objects the wrong way or in a way that harms the stability and strength of the spinal column. As I see it, some back pains are due to energy blockages resulting from the accumulation of mental and emotional tension, especially in the energy hubs of the spinal column. In cases where people complain of back pain, the bioenergetic treatment I administer is somewhat different from my normal treatment. Here, the patient lies on his stomach and the energy transfer focuses on the vertebrae; each vertebra is a separate energy unit with an energy hub—a chakra. By concentrating deeply during the treatment I find the energy hub, to which I transfer energy from the palms of my hands.

Where the problem is caused by inflammation, the bioenergetic treatment around the vertebrae causes the liquid at the point of local inflammation to be drained. As the pressure caused by the accumulation of liquids and the swelling around the edges of the vertebrae decreases, the pain is lessened. After the inflammation is down, the respective disk or vertebra returns spontaneously to its proper place. The patient's condition improves.

David Yitzhaki is a driving teacher by profession. He arrived at the clinic supported by two men. While he waited for his appointment, he had to stand up, leaning on the table. When I saw how he was suffering, I brought him in ahead of his turn. I realized that he was unable to sit or lie down, because the motion of bending his back brought about excruciating pain. With tremendous effort, David finally managed to lie down on the bed I use for such treatments. He had been suffering from terrible back pain for a very long time and was totally unable to function. Not long before he had consulted a medical specialist, who told him he needed to be operated on for a slipped disk. David refused and went to another specialist, who agreed with the first doctors and even set a date for the operation.

After my first bioenergetic treatment, David sat up on the bed and told me that the pain had decreased markedly. After the second and third treatments, he was already able to sit or lie down much more easily. As a result, he postponed his operation for a month. At the end of that month, when he went for a further examination prior to his surgery, the doctors were amazed at the tremendous improvement in his condition and agreed that an operation was not necessary. As I understand it, the transfer of energy caused the disk to return to its original place spontaneously.

Pain Without Physiological Cause

In our day-to-day lives, we are always influenced by the energies of tension, anger, excitement, and suffering, and these are absorbed by us without our being aware of it. In most cases, our natural defense system enables us to neutralize these negative energies and to filter them out of our bodies over the course of time. However, there are occasions when people accumulate these energies in various places in their bodies and "create" within their bodies real physical feelings of pain and suffering.

Some people have come to me complaining of inexplicable pain throughout their bodies or about pain in a specific region, even though all the medical tests have not shown any physical problems. The affected area may be unconsciously linked to a part of the body of profound spiritual and emotional significance in the patient's life. The source of pain will be the negative energy the person absorbed from his environment through the different chakras. Examples are migraine headaches, baffling strong heartbeats, difficulties in swallowing, and inexplicable stomach pains. In such cases, I divide the treatment into two stages: In the first stage, using bioenergetic treatment, I cleanse the aura, the chakras, and the meridians, and thus enable positive energy to flow into the body. The second stage, though, depends on whether the patient is willing to deal with his pain by thinking correctly and positively, thereby enabling the creation of a stronger electromagnetic field around the body and rejecting any accumulation of negative energies. The patient must understand the motives which caused him to retain the pain and must want with all his might to rid himself of it and to protect himself in the future. If the patient doesn't do it, the bioenergetic treatment is only good for a limited period of relief, and the pain will strike again.

A woman named Ruth came to my clinic at the request of her physician-husband, who had heard about me from a patient whom I had helped with his shoulder pains and who, as the result of my treatment, had not needed to undergo an operation. This story had impressed the doctor greatly, and so he decided to send his wife, who suffered from severe stomach pains for which no medical reason could be found. Ruth is a nurse by profession and works in a hospital. When she came to me with her complaint, I realized that in the course of her work and her encounters with the patients she treated, she had identified with their suffering and pain and had allowed energy saturated with pain and tension to enter her own energy field. Ruth's stomach pains disappeared totally after only a few treatments. Nevertheless, they do recur every so often. Ruth then receives further bioenergetic treatment, which she accepts understandingly, and the pains disappear for a considerable period of time.

Ear and Hearing Problems

Hearing problems and severe ear inflammation can be caused by energy blockages. Many patients, including a large number of children, arrive at the clinic suffering from chronic ear inflammation. In the course of the bioenergetic treatment, there is a sudden gush of liquid from the ears. In other instances there is a discharge of what appears to be a congealed liquid. When I move my hands above the ears of the patient, this takes place. Just before this happens, patients report a feeling like ants crawling or a strong itch in the ear. Usually, the inflammation disappears completely.

As to hearing difficulties, one of my most dramatic cases concerns a boy named Zvika. Zvika was about seven or eight years old when he came to the clinic at the end of 1988. Zvika lived in the United States with his parents and had come to visit his family in Israel. He was accompanied by his aunt and grandmother.

The two women told me that Zvika was severely hearing impaired, with no hearing at all in one ear and only 20 percent hearing in the other. While he had been born without any hearing difficulties, a disease a few years earlier had impaired his hearing. He was attending a special school because of his impairment. He kept looking around at me and the room, then lay down on the treatment bed, with his aunt and grandmother watching what was taking place. His eyes followed the palms of my hands as they moved above him; his gaze was one of tense expectancy. Soon liquid began to flow from Zvika's ears; I continued to direct energy into his energy hubs. Most of Zvika's communication took the form of lipreading, but during the treatment I suddenly asked, "What is your name?" He answered, "Zvika." "Were do you live?" Zvika answered me. I now asked him to block his relatively good ear with his fingers and continued to ask him questions while standing behind him. He kept answering me, as if hearing through the ear with the total hearing loss. I saw Zvika three or four times after this, and each time his hearing showed improvement. He returned to his home in the United States, where it was determined that his hearing had indeed improved dramatically and amazingly. He then underwent various medical tests, but the doctors were unable to find any reason for what had happened, for the problematic internal structure of the ear had remained unchanged. Zvika was transferred to a regular school.

In the weekly *The World of Fashion* of July 1989, Esther Tal, a journalist, described her experiences when she visited me: "For many long months I suffered with earaches that drove me crazy. I would suddenly experience an attack, without any prior notice. There were different types of pain: dull, strong, or sharp as a knife, accompanied by tremendous itching. The ear, nose, and throat doctor of our medical fund gave me various ointments and drops, but nothing helped. I went to Ze'ev Kolman. I lay down on his treatment bed. Ze'ev passed his hands over my ears, moving them alternatively closer and further. I felt a strong itching in my left ear, as if a colony of ants had taken refuge in it. It was a very strange sensation which is difficult to define. After treating the ear, Ze'ev moved over to treat the sinuses and placed two fingers on my forehead; I then felt gentle electric currents circulating near my nose. He passed his hands over my face, and I felt as if a soft brush was stroking my body and was hovering over it. I felt a deep sense of relief and concentrated on the pleasant sensations. Suddenly he said, 'Look at the pillow; all of the congealed matter came out of your ear and soaked the pillow.' I saw a puddle on the pillow. Where my ear had rested, there was a wet stain. I felt a tremendous sense of relief in my ear, as if a large cork which had been blocking it had been removed. For about a month now, I have not felt any pain in my left ear. This is what I experienced; the pain is gone."

Eye Problems

Sometime in 1986 a woman called Sarai told me about a man named Adam whose eyesight had not improved in spite of intensive medical care; he lived in a house in one of the suburbs of Tel Aviv, and even though he had a beautiful garden surrounding the house, his physical state precluded his entering the garden and enjoying its plants. He was a computer programmer by profession. I expressed reservations about my ability to help the man and indicated that I did not want to build up any false hopes. But Sarai begged me to try, and in the end she persuaded me to visit Adam with her. After we were introduced, Adam sat down and I began moving my hands above him, concentrating intently as I placed my hands over his eyes. At first he did not react at all. I repeated the action over and over for some time, and eventually he reported he felt an itching and the crawling of ants as the energy entered his eyes. Suddenly, he turned to me and cried out, "I see a shadow! I see a shadow!" I stopped the treatment for a short time in order to allow Adam to rest and to control his emotions. After a few minutes we continued with the treatment, as I transferred to his eyes the energy that flowed through me. Suddenly, his face reddened, his breathing became easier, and he exclaimed, "I see better and better!" I continued until I felt that his body was not absorbing any more energy. Adam got up and insisted we drink a toast and have some cake, and he went over to the kitchen to prepare these. A week later I came again to Adam's house with Sarai. This time one of Adam's friends was sitting in the living room. At Adam's request I treated him in the presence of the friend. The treatment was very successful; Adam's vision was returning.

Asthma and Other Breathing Difficulties

A woman by the name of Hannah Z. offers this testimonial of her experience: "For an extended period of time I had suffered from a cough similar to asthma. I literally felt that I had insufficient oxygen in the chest. You treated me a few times, and only through the help of your hands, without touching anything, my breathing has become clear and regular. I feel a tremendous amount of relief and I breathe clear air. I find it hard to understand how such a thing happens, because no doctor helped, and only you did so without any medications."

Another asthma case concerns a relative of mine named Howard F., of Netanya, who was about ten years old at the time; the year was 1980. During a visit with Howard's parents, they told me he suffered from terrible asthma attacks. That very evening I gave the child a bioenergetic treatment. Immediately after the treatment Howard felt a little better, but he did not feel any substantial change. The next morning, though, on the way to school he was overcome by nausea and threw up. As he went on, he threw up phlegm and mucus a number of times. He returned home, feeling terrible, but his breathing was normal. Since then, he has breathed without any problem.

Strokes

In most cases the time for successful bioenergetic treatment is as soon as possible after the stroke. In cases where a lengthy period of time had passed after the stroke, the percentage of those whom I was able to help was much lower. It is possible that the energy which flows into the brain through the chakras causes blood clots to dissolve.

Yossi Ofir of Rehovot wrote to me in 1984: "About a month ago, my father was hospitalized at the Kaplan Hospital because of a blood clot in the brain. On Saturday night his situation became extremely critical; he was unconscious and we knew that his days were numbered. Out of desperation, without any great hope, I called you for your aid. In spite of the lateness of the hour, you agreed to come and examine my father. After remaining alone with my father for about 15 minutes, you came out and said, 'Tomorrow he will be fine.' To my amazement, my father came to the next morning, woke up, and left the hospital about a week later."

Problems with the Functioning of the Limbs

David Hen, of Kfar Habad, came to me suffering from problems with the fingers of his right hand, which limited him greatly and prevented him from engaging in his occupation as a cook. After two treatments his hand returned to normal and he was able to run his cutting machines, something he had been unable to do until then. I sent most of my energy into the joints of his fingers, and his pain totally disappeared.

Yitzhak Glaser, a resident of Rishon-le-Zion, arrived suffering tremendous pain in his right shoulder, unable to lift his hand, even minimally. As the doctors had recommended an operation, he decided to try his luck with alternative medicine in my clinic. Indeed, after a number of treatments his shoulder returned to its normal condition, without pain and without the need for an operation.

Disturbances in Women's Reproductive Systems

Many women have come to me because they have stopped having a monthly period and there is no medical explanation for it. Generally, a single treatment or a few treatments are enough to realign the hormones properly. Incidentally, the women with this type of disorder have been of various ages, ranging from seventeen to forty.

During the treatment I pass my hands over the chakra of the lower abdomen and over the sex chakra [a little above the sex organs], at a distance so that the body can absorb the energy. The cleansing of the chakras and the refilling of them with renewed energy permits the flow of the correct energy to the reproductive organs. The women who undergo this treatment report a feeling of movement in the abdomen and in the pelvic region, a feeling similar to that of a mixer churning inside them, as my hands move in circles. Some of them report a feeling of internal warmth in the abdomen. In most cases the woman's period begins again and becomes as regular as it was before the disturbance. This particular condition is one of those most likely to respond to bioenergetic treatment.

As to disturbances in reproduction and the failure of a woman to become pregnant, there was one case involving spiritual guidance. A certain woman named Bilhah Gergi, who was very religious, came to me because for nine years she had been unable to conceive as a result of an abortion that she had undergone, this following a pregnancy which occurred almost immediately after her having given birth, and she had felt that the second pregnancy was too early. Some time later she attempted again to conceive, and since that time she had been unsuccessful; all medical treatments had failed her.

During the first treatment, she reported to me feelings of turning and churning within her abdomen. During one of the next treatments, I was impelled to state, "You are pregnant!" She smiled cynically and answered, "It can't be, because I was already pregnant before and I know what if feels like. Had I been pregnant, I would have known and felt it!" In spite of the cynicism in her voice, there was something within me that caused me to go on. "You are pregnant and you will have a daughter who will be born on Israel's Independence Day!" But the doubts on her face did not disappear. Then Bilhah telephoned me to inform me that tests had shown that she was indeed pregnant! For a long time thereafter I did not hear from her. The day after Independence Day, Bilhah called from the hospital to inform me that she had indeed given birth to a daughter on the date I had told her.

Mental Illness

Mental illness, and certain behavior which medicine considers to be psychotic, I believe to be spiritual disturbances.

A certain young woman came to the clinic and told me that she had been hospitalized in the Abarbanel Psychiatric Hospital in Bat Yam after having undergone numerous psychological and psychiatric tests. At the time she was still taking large quantities of psychiatric drugs daily. As I observed her aura, I remember that it was very weak and thin, of a dirty white and yellow color, indicating mental problems. Why had she been hospitalized? Sometimes, when she slept, she felt accompanied by tremendous fear that she might not be able to return to her body after leaving it during sleep. This fear prevented her from falling asleep at night.

After being subjected to various tests, she had been given a large quantity of tranquilizers and sleeping pills to help her sleep more soundly. But as a result of the medication she was receiving, she walked about during the day apathetic and in a stupor; she had stopped working, her lifestyle had changed completely, and her daily functioning in other areas also decreased markedly. She had been suffering this way for a number of years, but in the year preceding her visit to the clinic the "exits from her body" had increased, and these, in turn, had intensified her fear. After she asked the medical profession for help, it was decided to hospitalize her. About a month later she called me. "Thanks to our meeting, the amount of medication I am taking has been reduced drastically and I have gone back to work."

Ze'ev will take on cases generally considered the province of psychiatrists, and because he deals with them precisely the way he deals with physical ailments, he often has succeeded in relieving the problems. Because Ze'ev considers all illness spiritually connected, dealing with the aura and applying his bioenergetic power to it would seem to be as valid for emotional or mental disturbances as it is for purely physical problems.

This is the more important because a majority of conventional psychiatrists still refuse to consider the existence of an etheric inner body or continuance of life beyond physical death. Consequently, numerous patients reporting what are truly psychic disturbances are being railroaded into conventional treatments with therapy, drugs, or worse, which neither help the problem nor address it properly.

To be sure, there is insanity and psychosis, and they need to be treated accordingly. But the experience of an apparition of the "dead," or an out-of-body experience, or the hearing of voices of someone known to be deceased or at a distance are standard phenomena well known to parapsychology and are not hallucinations or incidents of madness.

11

Cancer

No disease is more feared than cancer, and no disease is less understood by conventional medicine. Because cancer research is not breaking new ground despite the huge sums of money spent on research, something may be basically wrong with the approach taken toward its conquest.

Could it not be, many in the field of alternative medicine postulate, that cancer is not a disease at all, but a form of malfunctioning of the bodily immune system, of the physical structure called body? Instead of searching for a virus or other external cause underlying the unwanted cell growth that is at the heart of all cancers, should not the cause be found in the person's individual situation on the three levels of body, mind, and—ah—spirit?

Already some progressive medical doctors realize that emotions, thoughts, or environment may well be the culprits, and no pill or surgeon's knife is going to deal with that. We seem to overlook the causative factors of long-term food poisoning—diets containing additives and toxic matter; we shrug off the environmental poisoning as too difficult to undo under our modern economic system; and most of us refuse to accept the notion that we do have an energy body within the physical, outer layer we ordinarily consider the seat of our personality, our self. Only Cayce, among modern healers, understood the concept of the energy body, and to this day the Cayce clinic in Phoenix, Arizona, deals with patients from that point of view.

Ze'ev knows that energy fields are what he deals with, too—that of both the patient and the power flowing from his healing hands. By replacing the damaged portion of the patient's energy field with fresh, powerful bioenergy from his own body and interior energy field, Ze'ev attacks the end result of the disease we call cancer. Sometimes he meets it early on, when it has not yet done too much damage, and sometimes he is called in when chances are dim for positive results, either because too much time has passed or because conventional treatments have weakened the patient's physical body so it cannot fully absorb the powerful bioenergetic treatment any longer.

It is in this, Ze'ev's approach to healing cancer, that hope lies, not in radiation and chemotherapeutic attack. The latter destroys more than it cures, while bioenergetic treatment has no side effects whatever and often cures the patient. This, coupled with healthful diet, is the answer. Over the years, Ze'ev has come to terms with the dreaded enemy, he has gotten to know it pretty well, and he has his own ideas, based on his experiences, as to what causes the disease in the first place.

Today, in the United States, Ze'ev has an impressive track record of accomplished cancer cures, well attested to medically and clinically. In Israel, in the early years, he had not yet entered into the limelight where medical people would begin to notice him and take him seriously.

Encounters with cancer have been numerous in my clinic. Cancer appears in visible form a long time after it has begun incubating in the body, years before one becomes aware of the disease. The first signs of cancer are an unexplained weakness and emotional tension, weariness, and a desire to sleep more. A most traumatic and problematic process occurs when the cancer is detected by conventional medicine, and the emotional shock brings about a worsening of the condition. Cancer feeds on tension, distress, suffering, feelings of desperation, and the emotional trauma involved. I attach a great deal of importance to the thought patterns of the patient. Even though disease and suffering are linked to one's karma, events in our lives and the way we deal with them contribute considerably to the development of cancer.

Eighty percent of all cancers stem from emotional causes, and in this sense one can say that the disease is in essence psychosomatic. Only 20 percent of cases have an organic, possibly genetic basis.

Over the years I have found that people with a specific type of cancer have experienced a specific type of emotional trauma in their lives. For example, most of those suffering with cancer of the thyroid are males, and in all the cases in my clinic these were men who had been divorced against their will. From this I deduced that this specific trauma brings about a tendency to develop this disease specifically in the region of the throat. I find it hard to explain how this occurs and why, but this is what I observed time and time again.

When a patient sits down opposite me, I look at the aura around his head and body. If I see stains of an orange-red color, scattered at various points of the aura, they are an indication that the person either has a cancer or at least an inflammation.

Navah Ruhan, a patient, came back with her husband's father who was suffering from tiredness and weakness as well as from unexplained pains. I looked at his aura. His aura was white, with a blue border, but at the right side of his head, above the ear, there was a reddish enlarged bean-shaped stain, which I interpreted as an infection of the liver or cancer in that organ. I told Navah that her father-in-law had a serious problem with his liver and to take him to a hospital as soon as possible to have a specialist examine him. Two weeks later, Navah called and told me that medical tests had shown what I had indicated.

When a cancer patient decides to seek bioenergetic treatment, he often comes to me at a stage where he is beyond hope. The first meeting with cancer patients is therefore a very difficult one. The patient expects miracles and has no idea whatsoever as to what to expect. In most cases, bioenergy is not a substitute for conventional medical treatment. When medicine has no other solutions to offer the patient, bioenergetic treatment offers another approach. But I cannot help every person. In a few cases I was able to effect a real cure. In others it was a temporary remission for a limited time or a decrease in the degree of suffering. In other patients I have not been able to help at all. Lessening the patient's suffering depends on how far the disease has spread when he comes to the clinic, that is, whether the cancer is at the beginning or in an advanced state.

The success rate of bioenergetic treatment is higher before chemotherapeutic treatment. I suffer physically when I deal with a patient who has undergone radiation or chemotherapy. When I pass my hands over such a patient, I often feel giddiness and nausea, because the energy waste seems to pass through me. These feelings make things much more difficult. In any event, in terminal cases the real aid I can offer is in granting the possibility to the terminally ill person of ending his life with less suffering and fewer narcotics. I attach great importance to the fact that a person who suffers so tremendously from pain should have a minimal control of his life, and he should not lose his image as a human being as he deteriorates as a result of the disease. In spite of my seeming pessimism about the disease, I believe with all my heart that it is in the power of one's thoughts and emotions to affect the condition and on occasion even to halt it and extend life expectancy.

It is most important to work on one's emotions, with the aim of avoiding, if possible, tension and of dealing with frustrations by the use of one's imaginative powers. In other words, the sick person must imagine and see himself in his mind's eye as functioning normally, feeling well, and overcoming the disease. Such a positive perception can influence the disease. The person who is ill should live as normally as possible, as an antithesis to the anxiety which paralyzes and aggravates the disease. Our life span is, in any event, ordained and beyond our control; we have to live to the best of our ability, without having control of the physical death which awaits us regardless. As our body is the temple of the soul, we should treat it with care. I have advised people to adopt a vegetarian diet and to drink only natural liquids for a period of three months while taking care to drink a great deal and to refrain from eating food which takes a long time for the body to digest, such as beef or other meat. During the time people undergo chemotherapy, even though they generally lose their appetite, I have suggested they continue to eat planned meals with small quantities of food several times during the day and to be sure to drink liquids at least once every hour.

A woman named Alona came to the clinic in 1986 with her husband, who suffered from numbness in his leg. I offered to try and help him. On one occasion, when her husband came for treatment, Alona entered the treatment room also. I looked at her aura and suddenly saw above her left eye a reddish violet stain, from which a clear avocado-colored cord extended to the chest area. I felt this suggested a nonmalignant growth in the breast. Spontaneously, I spread my hands toward her and told her that she had a growth in the breast, but it was not malignant. Her eyes showed amazement; she was scheduled to undergo an operation during the coming December to remove a nonmalignant growth the size of a tangerine, her doctors had told her. Alona asked whether I could help her.

After three months of bioenergetic treatments, Alona went to the hospital and found herself on the operating table. The surgeon arrived and began to look for the growth but was amazed to find nothing there. Alona was removed from the operating table, and the mammography she underwent afterwards showed that the growth was smaller than an almond. It had miraculously shrunk. The doctors decided that there was no need for the operation. Three years have passed since then, and Alona's health is excellent.

I saw Tzali Zigmond for the first time being carried by two men. He looked emaciated, and his face expressed pain and suffering. Tzali was brought into my clinic and was placed on the treatment bed. There was a massive scar on his head from an operation he had undergone a month earlier, the head completely bald due to chemotherapy. I began to radiate energy into his entire body, from the large energy hubs to the small ones and back again, from his feet to the central chakra of the head. Afterwards, the treatment concentrated on his maimed head. Wherever I radiated energy, Tzali reacted by moving different parts of his body. The color of his face changed, the paleness disappeared, and his cheeks took on a faint blush. After the first treatment, Tzali got off the bed on his own and walked unassisted from the clinic; he appeared to have been rejuvenated. From one session to the next, his weight increased and his face filled out.

Some time later Tzali and his wife left for a tour of Holland. When they returned I saw that he was full of vigor, and he was again functioning fully at the factory at which he had worked previously. He felt that his stamina was returning and that he was on the right path. But sometime later, unfortunately, Tzali's cancer had spread to the liver. I treated him again, and after four or five bioenergetic sessions, Tzali's doctors were amazed that there was no longer cancer in the liver, without any rational medical reason for this.

But they decided that Tzali was to receive a new kind of chemotherapy. Some time after this had begun, he came to the clinic for a bioenergetic treatment. This time I felt something like a prick as my hand passed over his head, a feeling which I had not noticed before. After medical tests it was found that the growth in his head had begun acting up again. The doctors suggested that Tzali undergo another operation. Tzali underwent the operation and the growth was removed, but as a result his brain was affected and his entire body deteriorated markedly, making it difficult for him to speak. His condition worsened from day to day and he lost his will to live. Tzali was placed into a convalescent home for continued treatment. He died soon after.

When Tzali entered my clinic, he had been given but two months to live. Yet, he managed to live for another year and a half in which he experienced life to the fullest.

When conventional cancer therapy is used, it makes the bioenergetic treatment almost always null and void in the end. The philosophy behind the two methods is mutually exclusive and can lead only to counterproductive results. But until treatments like bioenergy are more fully understood and accepted by the medical fraternity, doctors as well as patients are likely to try the "devil they know" first, before turning to the "devil" they don't know. It takes courage and a greater knowledge of what is involved in the treatment process for a patient (and a doctor) to set aside old fears and prejudices regarding alternative methods and to allow a choice.

In my view, based on familiarity with many cases, chemotherapy and radiation prolong life but do not cure anything. On the other hand, by severely attacking the body's own natural defenses and destroying some of them in the process, such therapies make it all but impossible for the alternative approach to be successful. That Ze'ev even tries to treat a patient who has already had chemotherapy and surgery speaks highly for him; he isn't playing it safe at all.

12

The Kolman Method:
How It Works

Discussing the results of the healing sessions, especially when they are beneficial in their results, is most important; the end result is all a patient looks forward to when consulting a paranormal healer. But to get a handle on what works, and how, we need to examine the system as well as the results.

I have long discovered that psychics and healers each have their own way of doing things and know what method works best for them. A lot has to do with their comfort levels, is certainly psychologically motivated, and is not necessarily the only, correct, or standard way of doing this kind of work. But it would be a grave mistake for investigators to impose their own sets of rules or to try and squeeze every subject into a framework created or approved by the appropriate scientific community. Yet, that is what, unfortunately, some more conservative scientific investigators of the paranormal like to do, with the results of their research being the poorer. Spontaneous attitudes on the part of the psychic or healer are to be encouraged so long as we are able to properly and carefully monitor them and approach the results with an open-minded, scientific attitude.

Apparently, the way Ze'ev works does not present any problems of acceptance by an unbiased scientific investigator. He starts the session with a patient by sitting opposite and engaging him or her in relaxing conversation. Getting the patient to relax is important because, according to Ze'ev, a nervous person's aura appears distorted and prevents his interpretation and thus the healing. Ze'ev accomplishes this by talking about anything but the illness or problem that has brought the patient to seek him out. Imagine a medical doctor following this method!

Ze'ev likes to have flowers in the room and New Age–type background music as further inducements to full relaxation. When the patient is relaxed and Ze'ev is able to study the aura to see where the energy field is weak or missing, the real healing session begins. Wherever Ze'ev sees the problem in the aura, there he will concentrate his healing. He places the patient on his work table and begins his work from a distance of about two feet. For a few moments he is silent as he places himself into a state of light trance. When he feels he has reached it, he then begins to pass his open palms in broad strokes over the patient's body, always staying more or less the same distance away. The healing is meant to touch the outer limit of the patient's aura, not the skin. Only now and then does Ze'ev actually touch the patient's principal trouble spot, usually at the end of the session. If the patient's body is very sick or the patient is old, he may approach the aura a little more closely so as to increase the radiation emanating from the palms of his hands.

He tries to pour fresh energy into the areas of the aura in need of it and to equalize the field so as to restore the patient's healthy status. At the same time he removes from the body the toxic energy, the portion of the weakened aura that in his view is the cause of the problem.

What exactly does Ze'ev see when this is going on, and does he feel anything special? He does see light coming from his fingers, and he sees the chakras or energy centers in the patient's aura—making the point that the auric chakras, not their physical portions in the body itself, are to be dealt with. He feels the presence and influence of his spirit guides when he does this work and confirms that his hands just move along to the right areas as if controlled by his guides. He can make out colors—blue, purple, yellow, green—that he calls the "good" colors; he continues to pump energy into the patient's body (and aura) until he knows the body cannot absorb anything further, and then he stops.

He next places a shield of protection around the patient's body. This blue, purple, and white layer of protection is to prevent a recurrence, if possible, of the illness or disturbance. Such a shield is nothing more than additional bioenergy placed around the now detoxified aura of the person being treated. According to Ze'ev, the negative energy removed from the patient's aura goes off into the ether—the atmosphere—to the right side of the patient, whereas the positive energy, the healing force, approaches the patient from the left side.

In addition, there are definite physical sensations the patient experiences during the healing: heat, a prickly sensation, needlelike stabs, a windlike air current passing over the affected area getting the healing, and sometimes water or other liquid emanating from the body, usually followed by the cure or a much better health condition, as if some toxic liquid had been eliminated. I can vouch for this, having undergone a number of such treatments and experiencing all these sensations. In some cases, when the ailment is deep inside the patient's body, the patient has reported feeling Ze'ev's hand inside—when of course it never enters the physical body. But his etheric hand may well do so.

The effects of a healing session can last for days or weeks, but usually more than one session is required for final results. Each case has its own requirement, which is dictated only by the ongoing status of the patient and no other considerations that are so common in conventional medicine, which frequently demand routine treatments and tests according to standards that never take into account an individual's rate of progress.

Self-healing is encouraged, and Ze'ev teaches his method to those willing to learn. Self-healing begins when Ze'ev's ministrations end.

After treating each patient, in order to protect his health, Ze'ev carefully washes his hands and creates a "Blue Shield" for himself before seeing the next caller (see page 170). He has no particular ritual other than early morning meditation, which he practices as part of his personal spiritual outlook and dedication.

Much as he acknowledges the influence of a Higher Power and of his spirit guides, Ze'ev is also a realist. He knows that the mechanical aspect of his healing lies in bioenergetic forces drawn from his body through the palms of his hands. In this sense his powers rely on the scientific understanding of all energy and how it works. In no way does it require suspension of disbelief or other kind of special commitment other than an open-minded attitude toward what is essentially a natural, human phenomenon partaking of a special gift he has developed.

Because it all started with a specific incident involving an encounter with extraterrestrials, we may wonder about those who had seemingly detained him for five hours and left him a fabulous healer. Was it all planned by them? Was it accidental? Similar encounters have been recorded, and some have turned the recipient of those experiences into highly charged psychic individuals, whereas before the event there was no such ability.

If the incident was planned by what is surely a superior intelligence (at least technologically), then would those humanoids monitor the results of their visit? This sometimes happens. And indeed, there was an incident during a convention of environmentalists in Salzburg, Austria, in September 1992, which leads me to believe there was indeed a second encounter, though of a different kind.

During that short stay in Salzburg, Ze'ev was literally drawn from his hotel room to a window to observe what to him seemed a very unusual light in the sky, for which there was no ordinary explanation as to the source. However, there is nothing more concrete to report, at least not yet. It is a moot question whether the visitors from another world are watching what Ze'ev does. What is factual are the results of their initial contact with the man.

This link I consider very real, based not only on Ze'ev's testimony, but also by comparing the details with other, related incidents of this kind. I don't think that in 1995 properly reported incidents involving humanoids can be dismissed as fantasies or hallucinations. We are indeed not alone. Regrettably, it appears to me that a powerful technique of healing known to the strangers cannot as yet be shared fully and regularly with us and pops up only now and again in situations like Ze'ev's encounter in the Sinai Desert.

13

Kolman in America

The year 1989 marked a turning point in Ze'ev's professional life. His world began to encompass a different kind of crowd, both in his contacts and his surroundings. He had come to offer healing in the United States. Gradually, he realized that this was all meant to be, and he accepted his mission even though it puzzled him at times: Why me? But then he recalled the strange incident in the Sinai.

In Israel he had become well-known as a significant psychic healer, and even doctors at times referred their patients to him, especially when they had run out of solutions for their patients' problems. In the United States, however, he was an unknown quantity. Whereas in Israel a bioenergetic healer is a rarity, in the United States there are all kinds of paranormal healers—good, bad, and indifferent—but, it eventually turned out, none even remotely like Ze'ev.

To be sure, Ze'ev had performed so-called miracles in Israel, healing people sometimes spontaneously. To him they were no miracles but the result of Divine Guidance and his bioenergetic healing abilities. Perhaps one of his most significant cases of spontaneous healing, however, involved a man in the United States who had never heard of him and had absolutely no interest or belief in the power of bioenergetic healing—about as far as one can go from the world of faithful believers and preconditioned followers of the miraculous and the world of paranormal phenomena.

The subject of this case was Joseph Lavi, a businessman born in Haifa, Israel, in 1952. Mr. Lavi had served in the army, had spent two years at Columbia University in New York City, and had received a master's degree from the Technical University of Haifa. He had been director of marketing for a major bank, but in 1984 he had gone into business on his own. This had taken him to the United States, where he has lived ever since.

In January 1989, while on his way to a business meeting, Mr. Lavi was sitting in his car, stopped for a red light. At that moment he was hit from the rear by three cars, and as a result wound up with two herniated disks; he could no longer walk. He spent several months in a New York City hospital. There he was told that he had suffered, in addition to the two herniated disks, damage to his spinal nerve and that an operation was the only approach, although the chance of success was no more than 60 percent. He was in constant pain, could not go to the toilet unaided, and was utterly depressed by this prognosis.

Mr. Lavi received a telephone call from a friend familiar with his condition. She informed him that an Israeli healer named Ze'ev

Kolman was in New York City and that he should consult him. But Mr. Lavi refused; he had no faith in such people. The friend insisted, and in the end he agreed to visit Ze'ev, who was then staying at a relative's house. In 1989, Ze'ev had not yet started to do any healing in the United States and was here only for a visit.

Mr. Lavi was brought in his wheelchair, and Ze'ev started to treat him. At first, Mr. Lavi felt nothing special, but after a while he began to feel pinpricks as if he were stung by many needles. Being in a business specializing in technical inventions, he immediately assumed that Ze'ev was using some kind of gadget to produce the effects he felt on his body. Grabbing Ze'ev's hands quickly, he demanded to know what kind of electrical gadget Ze'ev had to produce the pinpricks. But, of course, he found nothing.

The healing session continued for about twenty minutes, then the treatment and the pinpricks stopped. Mr. Lavi asked his friend to bring him his wheelchair. Instead, Ze'ev ordered him to get up and walk.

Still doubtful, Mr. Lavi grabbed one leg, then the other, and for the first time he had feeling in his legs again; they had been totally numb for all those months. Next thing he knew he was standing, then walking, then running around the room. He did this for five minutes, and he could still walk!

Mr. Lavi had a hospital appointment a few days later. Dr. P. H., his surgeon, was puzzled when he saw Mr. Lavi walking into his office. Had the operation been performed? But then he realized it had not. When Mr. Lavi informed him of his visit to Ze'ev, the doctor was visibly upset and without further questioning asked him to leave the hospital.

Mr. Lavi had been handed back his life, so to speak, and he went about his business as he had done before the unfortunate accident. There was no further trouble with his legs. He visited Ze'ev a couple of times more anyway, even though he was fine. Then Ze'ev went back to Israel. Impressed with what had happened to him, Mr. Lavi tried to convince Ze'ev to work in the United States, but he refused, citing his many commitments to his patients in Israel and to his family there.

Nine months later, Mr. Lavi had another accident near his home in New Jersey. In the dead of winter he slipped on the ice, and once again his legs became paralyzed. While being carried into his house, he thought, If only Ze'ev Kolman were here now, he could help me. Ten minutes later the telephone rang. It was Ze'ev, calling at three in the morning Israel time.

"What's wrong with you?" he demanded, and immediately Mr. Lavi thought that one of his friends must have contacted Ze'ev about the new accident. But, of course, nobody had.

After learning what had occurred, Ze'ev told Mr. Lavi to relax and hold on to the telephone, and Ze'ev would heal long-distance. As ordered, Mr. Lavi laid down on his stomach. Within minutes he felt a heat wave envelop his back.

"You'll be all right again in ten minutes," Ze'ev said, and went back to bed.

Fifteen minutes after this conversation, Mr. Lavi got up and walked normally as if nothing had happened to him.

The experience with Ze'ev left an indelible mark on former skeptic Joseph Lavi. When his business partner's child was diagnosed as autistic, Mr. Lavi offered help. The boy was eight months old when he was diagnosed. At first the father was adamant; after all, the medical doctors had given him no hope. But Mr. Lavi persuaded his partner to fly Ze'ev to New York, and Ze'ev came for two weeks. After that time and with intensive treatments, the boy began to show signs of improvement: he began to take an interest in his surroundings. Five-and-a-half years later, the boy attended a regular kindergarten. He is just fine.

The boy's father helped Mr. Lavi persuade Ze'ev to stay in New York, at least part time. Being in real estate, he was able to provide Ze'ev with accommodations in the city. Ze'ev was on his way to becoming known here and, in time, an international force trying to help those who seek him out. He was now a man with many countries where he could help people.

There was very little publicity then, primarily word of mouth from those he had helped. In 1990, Ira, a veteran of the Vietnam War, came in the hope of obtaining relief because medical doctors had failed him. Ira had been exposed to the infamous Agent Orange, and the poison dioxin had caused his immune system to break down, leaving him in a toxic condition. A tumor on his shoulder would not yield to conventional treatments. After the first session with Ze'ev, which lasted about twenty-five minutes, Ira felt cleansed, in a way, and after the third session the tumor had become much softer and smaller. During Ze'ev's ministrations, as he passed his hands above Ira's body, Ira responded strongly, even going into a kind of muscular seizure as his body moved up and down rapidly when the bioenergetic force was applied. Ira is well now.

14

Documented Cases
of Healing

In 1990, Ze'ev met Ricardo Cisneros, a Venezuelan businessman who had heard of his healing work. Mr. Cisneros heads up a major television network as well as Spaulding USA, the sports company, and is a respected leader in the community. In 1993, Victor Mateo, the cousin of one of his executives, was diagnosed with terminal cancer of the spine and was given only several months to live. Ze'ev, nevertheless, treated the man for a week. As a result he was totally free of cancer by the fall of that year and still is today.

Not all cases can be fully documented with medical reports and laboratory tests, but this is one which has that distinction. From March 30, 1993, through August 2, 1993, the reports and tests clearly demonstrate the presence and diagnosis of the disease and its elimination.

We may not know the exact mechanics of how Ze'ev's bio-energetic powers affect the cancer or the details of what they do to the malignant cells, but the result is often, and certainly in the Victor Mateo case, the elimination of the cancer process. Because electrical forces are always involved in all living tissue, could it not be that the powerful bioenergy applied through Ze'ev's hands has simply overcome the energy of the malignant cells and has replaced the "bad" energy field with positive particles?

On the following pages are the documents demonstrating the results of the clinical work done on Mr. Mateo.

RICARDO CANNKINEN

October 19, 1993

Professor Hans Holzer
140 Riverside Drive
New York, N.Y. 10024

Dear Professor Holzer,

Zeev Kolman is an extraordinary person that appears once in a millenium. Zeev is full of love, almost childish for all of mankind and has the gift of tapping into the universal forces to harness this love into a potent healing and regenerating force.

I have brought to Zeev's attention and healing Victor Mateo, who has been diagnosed with a terminal cancer of the spine and had been given months to live. I am sending under separate cover all test results and the phisicians prognosis.

Victor today, after a weeks' sessions with Zeev, is completely cured and cancer free.

For Zeev the only pleasure is one of helping others and he goes to incredible length to be of help.

Best regards,

SERVICIO DE LABORATORIO "POLICLINICA SANTIAGO DE LEON"

Emergencias y Domicilios - Avenida Libertador - Sabana Grande

Teléfono: 761.91.51 al 59 - Directo: 762.47.55

Paciente: *VICTOR MATEO.*

Fecha: *30-3-93*   Hab.: ....

LAB N° *23830*

GRUPO SANGUINEO ....

FACTOR RH ....

PROTROMBINA { PACIENTE: *13" = 84.9 %* CONTROL: *12" = 100 %*

P.T.T. { PACIENTE: *37"* CONTROL: *32"*

MONOTEST ....

RETRACCION DEL COAGULO ....

CELULAS L.E. ....

LATEX-RA TEST ....

PROT. C. REACTIVA *POSITIVO.*

V.D.R.L. CUALITATIVO ....

CUANTITATIVO ....

A.S.T.O. ....

ANTIGENOS FEBRILES {
EBERTH "H" ....
EBERTH "O" ....
PARA "A" ....
PARA "B" ....
PROTEUS OX 19 ....
BRUCELLA ABORTUS ....

BIOANALISTA

139

HOSPITAL DE CLINICAS CARACAS C.A.

Dpto. Anatomía Patológica
Solicitud de Examen

Dra. Paulina Apeloig de Altaras
Dr. Daniel Scharifker
Dra. Marleny Lunar de Uribe
Dra. Eva Zucker K.

Nº 16005

Nombre *Victor Mateu*   Edad   Sexo

Hospitalizado ☐   Habitación o Cama   Fecha y Hora   *02-06-93*

Ambulatorio ☑   Teléfono

Médico Referente - Dirección y Teléfono

BIOPSIA ☒ No.   CITOLOGIA ☐ No.

CODIGO									TIPO Y LUGAR DE LA MUESTRA
2	8	0	0						
2	8	0	0						
2	8	0	0						
2	8	0	0						
2	8	0	0						

DATOS CLINICOS E IMPRESION DIAGNOSTICA

Enfermedad de Hodgkin en estudio clínicamente IB -

Estudios Anatomopatológicos   Intervenciones Quirúrgicas, Tratamientos, Hormonales, Radio y/o Quimioterapeuticos.

HISTORIA GINECOLOGICA (SI ES APLICABLE)

F.U.R.	Partos	Abortos

Enfermera   Dr.

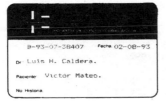

Nombre del Paciente:
MATEO VICTOR JOSE

Fecha:
29-07-93

SOLIC 3703 31 A.

DPTO. DE RADIOLOGIA

Dra. Carmen Hernandez H.
Dr. Carlos González Denis
Dr. Carlos Soto R.
Dr. Enrique Manuela I.
Dr. Gaston Vici S.
Dra. Mariela Salazar C.
Dr. Oscar Solis Q.
Dr. Sergio Tovar A.

"**INFORME RADIOLOGICO**"

Referido por Dr.   CALDERA LUIS HUMBERTO.

Rx. de   TAC DE CUELLO / TORAX / ABDOMEN Y PELVIS.

CONCLUSSION:

NO HAY EVIDENCIA TOMOGRAFICA QUE SUGIERA PRESENCIA DE
LA ENFERMEDAD A NIVEL DE CUELLO, TORAX, ABDOMEN Y PEL-
VIS.
SINUSOPATIA INFLAMATORIA MAXILAR *IZQUIERDA*.

DR.GASTON VICI S.

CGS/cy

B-93-07-38407   **Fecha** 02-08-93

Dr Luis H. Caldera.

Paciente Victor Mateo.

No Historia.

Departamento de Anatomía Patológica

Dra. Paulina Apeloig de Altaras.
Dr. Daniel Scharifker.
Dra. Marleny Lunar de Uribe.
Dra. Eva Zucker K.

MUESTRA:

Médula ósea.

DESCRIPCION MACROSCOPICA:

Cilindro de médula ósea de 3 cms. en longitud y 0.2 cms. en
diámetro. Se incluye completo previa decalcificación.

DESCRIPCION MICROSCOPICA:

Los cortes histológicos muestran una médula ósea normocelular con
elementos de todas las series hematopovéticas presentes, en
porciones normales y con maduración adecuada. Se ven escasos
plasmocitos. Se nota una parte del cilindro sin células
hematopovéticas o con muy pocas células linfoides y mieloides en
el tejido adiposo de los espacios intertrabeculares. Hay pequeñas
zonas de fibrosis. Las partes óseas tienen aspecto usual. No se
ven infiltrados neoplásicos, granulomas o necrosis.

DIAGNOSTICO:

MEDULA OSEA NORMOCELULAR.

EFECTOS POST QUIMIOTERAPIA.

NO SE VEN INFILTRADOS NEOPLASICOS.

DS/po.-

Dr. Daniel Scharifker.

Word of mouth is still the surest way for genuine psychics and successful healers to get attention for their work. So it was that Ricardo Cisneros's kindness in helping Victor Mateo came to the attention of others, among them Angelica García Sosa, who had been diagnosed with non-Hodgkin's lymphoma, a form of cancer. The treatments took place in New York City, where she saw Ze'ev for a series of eight treatments.

Here is her own statement and the supporting medical testimony.

Caracas, December 23,   1993

Mr. Zeev Kolman
New York

Dear Mr. Kolman:

Last year, in the month of June, I was diagnosed with a NO HODKIN LIMPOMA (spinal cord, colunn, and rectum), as can be clearly appreciated in the tests that were made on June 21, 1992.

For this reason I traveled to the city of New York where I was kindly attended by you, and at which time, eight (8) sessions of therapy were performed on me.

On my return to Caracas, I had to go onto a series of new tests and to my surprise the doctors found excellent response to the treatments I had been submitted to.

Enclosed please find copy of the reports supporting this information dated September 03, 1992, as well as the results of the BIOPSIA dated February 17, 1993, showing no alterations whatsoever on the spinal cord.

I gratefully thank you for the magnificent help you has given me, and sincerelly wish you all the best and a long and fruitful life so you can continue helping the needed ones.

All the best and a happy holiday season.

Regards,

Angelica García Sosa
Age: 59 years

June 21, 1992

HOSPITAL ONCOLOGICO PADRE MACHADO
SERVICIO DE PATOLOGIA

BIOPSIA NO : 3478-92

F/DE ENTRADA : 11/06/92   F/DE SALIDA : 21/06/92
NOMBRE : ANGELA GARCIA   SERVICIO : GASTRO
EDAD : 58 AÑOS   HC : 92.43.40
                                 DR : ▪=▪=

EXAMEN MACROSCOPICO :

RECTO :

Un (1) fragmento de tejido blanquecino, el mayor de 0,3 cms.
de diametro .

DIAGNOSTICO :

LINFOMA NO HODGKIN DIFUSO DE CELULAS PEQUEÑAS HENDIDAS(DE GRADO-
INTERMEDIO DE MALIGNIDAD) , CON NECROSIS, ULCERACION SUPERFICIAL
E INFLAMCION CRONICA REAGUDIZADA ; BIOPSIA DE RECTO .

DRA . ANTONIETA RENNOLA   DRA . BLENDA MORA .

ct ; 220692.

Hospital Oncológico Padre Machado
Servicio
Anatomía Patológica

143

September 3, 1992

**DEPARTAMENTO
DE DIAGNOSTICO
POR IMAGENES**

CENTRO MEDICO
DE CARACAS

Dr. Diego Núñez, hijo
Dra. Ana Bermúdez
Dra. Lilian Casas
Dr. José Antonio Cisneros
Dra. Gisela Schmitz de Henriquez
Dr. Bernardo Lander

Caracas, 03 de Septiembre de 1992

Paciente: ANGELICA E. GARCIA SOSA
Referida por la Dra. ANGELINA RODRIGUEZ
Estudio: TAC DE TORAX-ABDOMEN Y PELVIS

INFORME

Se practicó estudio tomográfico toraco-abdominal previa opacificación de la via digestiva por solución yodada, el mismo es comparado con el realizado en fecha 18 de Junio del 92.

A nivel abdominal hay desaparición completa de las masas adenopáticas encontradas a nivel del lecho peri-pancreático, así como desaparición de la imagen infiltrativa de tipo tumoral a nivel del ciego.

Tampoco se demuestran cambios significativos en el grosor de la pared del recto-sigmoides.

No hay ganglios retroperitoneales.

Permanecen sin cambios la morfología, tamaño y densidad del hígado y el bazo.

La exploración torácica no demuestra adenomegalias mediastínicas ni cambios significativos en la radiotransparencia pulmonar.

CONCLUSIONES:

Manifestaciones de excelente respuesta al tratamiento, actualmente sin criterios de actividad linfoproliferativa.

El estudio es considerado básicamente normal tanto a nivel torácico como abdomino-pélvico.

AG/gg.

Dra. Ana Gascue

144

February 17, 1993

Dr. PEDRO MORE BERICAT
PATOLOGO QUIRURGICO: Mount Sinai Hospital New York y Oncológico de Tokyo
Certificado American Board of Pathology
Miembro AIPDV, ASCP y CAP
Dr. RAMON PIÑANGO M.
CITOPATOLOGO: Hospital General Universidad Nacional de México
Miembro SVAP y SLAP

POLICLINICA
BARQUISIMETO

HISTOPATOLOGIA · CITOPATOLOGIA S.R.L.

| 17 | 02 | 93 |

BIOPSIA   57.721

GARCIA ANGELICA   58   F.
NOMBRE   EDAD   SEXO

                    ROGER FEBRES MENDEZ
HISTORIA No.   REFERIDO POR DR.   HAB.

MEDULA OSEA
ESPECIMEN

LINFOMA NO HODGKIN
RESUMEN CLINICO

El especimen en fijador consiste en un fragmento cilíndrico de tejido pardo de consistencia dura, de 1 x 0,1 cms.

Se procesó todo el material, previa decalcificación, obteniéndose 8 cortes para microscopía teñidos con HE.

Microscópicamente se observa médula ósea de arquitectura conservada, mayormente adiposa, con todas las series presentes y en maduración.

Comentario: No se observa infiltración tumoral.

Diagnóstico: Fragmento de médula ósea sin alteraciones significativas

Dr. Pedro Moré B.   Dr. Ramón Piñango M.

In a rare display of honest appraisal of Ze'ev's work and its success, another patient's attending specialist summarized her illness and the results of Ze'ev's bioenergetic treatments. The patient was Thelma Cela, whose husband was persuaded to send her to New York City by the indefatigable champion of bioenergetic healing, Ricardo Cisneros.

Dr. Julio C. Pita, the specialist, was attending a medical symposium in Caracas, where he met Mrs. Cela, the director of programs for the Diabetes Treatment Center at Mercy Hospital in Miami, Florida; both were dinner guests of Ricardo Cisneros, who spoke highly of Ze'ev's work. Because Mrs. Cela was suffering from multiple sclerosis, which is not yet a disease that conventional medicine can heal, she decided to try the bioenergetic treatment. The result was a vast improvement in her condition.

Mrs. Cela came to visit Ze'ev in November 1993. At that time she could not walk and her entire left side was paralyzed. Ze'ev decided to give her double sessions for a week, in view of the severity of her condition.

The day she finished happened to fall on Chanukah, the Jewish Festival of Lights, considered the commemoration of a miracle of sorts. In 165 B.C., the Jews under the command of Judas Maccabeus liberated Jerusalem and the temple from Syrian control. However, they found enough oil for the sacred lamp to be lit for only one day; still, it stayed lit for eight days. Ze'ev had long hoped that as a result of his healing work there would be "at least one miracle a day."

That day Mrs. Cela went to the hospital for a thorough checkup. The next day the telephone rang early in Ze'ev's place. "Ze'ev,"

Mrs. Cela said excitedly, "guess what? A Chanukah miracle has happened to me."

The miracle was that the hospital found no further evidence of multiple sclerosis.

The following documents include Dr. Pita's summation of the course of the disease and the treatment, including Ze'ev's ministrations.

JULIO C. PITA, JR., M.D.
ENDOCRINOLOGY · DIABETES · INTERNAL MEDICINE
DIPLOMATE, AMERICAN BOARDS
OF ENDOCRINOLOGY AND INTERNAL MEDICINE
FELLOW OF THE AMERICAN COLLEGE OF PHYSICIANS

TELEPHONE
854-5432

3661 SOUTH MIAMI AVENUE
MIAMI, FLORIDA 33133

January 10, 1994

Mr. Zeev Kolman
Bioenergetic Healing

Re: Thelma Cela
     Date of Birth: 12/30/62

Dear Mr. Kolman:

I simply wanted to summarize for you the medical status of Miss Thelma Cela, who you had the opportunity to treat recently. Miss Cela is a 31 year old, young lady who was first diagnosed as having multiple sclerosis in April of 1990 by Dr. Raul Lopez, neurologist at Mercy Hospital in Miami. She was then referred to the Baird Multiple Sclerosis Center at the Millard Fillmore Hospital in Buffalo, New York, where she was a part of the beta interferon trial for two years, receiving one injection intramuscularly a week, the last injection on May 28, 1993.

With respect to her disease, she has had several exacerbations, one in October of 1990 when she developed a sensory dysfunction, specifically, complete numbness from the neck down, requiring one month hospitalization for daily IV ACTH, and in April of 1991 she developed motor dysfunction with an inability to walk or grasp items that required, again, one month hospitalization for IV ACTH.

Her last exacerbation was sensory in nature, involving facial numbness extending into the left side of the scalp. This started in October of 1993 and has not improved since that time.

In October of 1993, I had the opportunity to go to Caracas, Venezuela, to participate in a symposium on insulin pump therapy in Type I diabetes. Miss Cela, who is the Program Director of the Diabetes Treatment Center here at Mercy Hospital, also attended this meeting. We had the opportunity to go for dinner at the home of Mr. Ricardo Cisneros, who kindly invited both Miss Cela, myself, and also Maria Elena Torres, a nurse from the Diabetes Treatment Center, who was also attending this meeting. Ricardo, who is a good friend, discussed, during our conversation, his experiences with your bioenergetic healing and how impressed he had been with

Mr. Zeev Kolman   Page 2

Re: Thelma Cela

the response of several individuals, including a lady in Caracas
who had multiple sclerosis. Upon the mention of someone receiving
this type of treatment for multiple sclerosis, Miss Cela became
extremely interested. Mr. Cisneros generously offered Thelma the
opportunity to meet and receive treatment from you when you were
going to be in New York in November of 1993. Again, this generous
gesture led to Miss Thelma Cela going, on November 15, 1993, to New
York to meet you and receive your treatment. After several
treatments between November 15th and November 19th, 1993 of your
bioenergetic healing, the numbness in this young lady's scalp and
face totally disappeared. Although there is no objective way of
measuring this young lady's improvement and it is totally subjective, it was a rather dramatic improvement in symptoms that this
young lady had had already for approximately one month prior to
going to New York City.

I, obviously, as a physician, cannot explain the improvement and a
skeptic would say that she was going to get better anyway at that
point or that because it is a subjective problem that this young
lady was simply impressed into feeling that she was better.
However, I know Thelma Cela very well and the symptoms were rather
well-described and present and I feel that in some manner your
healing resolved this sensory problem this young lady had due to
her multiple sclerosis. To the moment, she remains without any
further facial or scalp numbness.

                              Sincerely,

                              Julio C. Pita, Jr., M.D., F.A.C.P.

JCP:va

cc: Ricardo Cisneros

Dear Jenn

I hope this letter finds you both doing very well! I have been thinking about you and wanted to send this brief note to let you both know I'm doing fine. My visit in November is something I'll never forget and will always be grateful to Ricardo Cisneros for his generosity in getting my husband & me to New York to see you.

I've enclosed a picture that we took in November. My expression displays how happy I was to be there.

Jenn — you are in my thoughts everyday — thank you!!

Your friend.
Thelma Cela

Mrs. Nanmoku of Japan had been treated for recurring breast cancer three times, undergoing the standard treatment for the disease, with all the side effects causing her great suffering and discomfort. The doctors gave her no hope of recovery. She is the sister-in-law of a man that is the president of the One Hundred Club and a prominent businessman both in Japan and in California. He knew Ze'ev and suggested Ze'ev try to help.

After one visit with Mrs. Nanmoku in New York City, Ze'ev started a series of absent healing sessions, the first two via telephone and then twice a week when she "tuned in" to Ze'ev at set times. Thus, starting with the session of July 15, 1994, and going to November 24, 1994, Ze'ev treated her in this manner, and she reported to him what she felt and how it affected her condition. Bear in mind that at the same time she was still being given drug treatments for her condition, something that would make Ze'ev's work more difficult. But by early September she was able to resume many of her usual activities, and the pain and discomfort began to lessen.

Finally, on December 2, 1994, Mrs. Nanmoku's brother-in-law sent a memo advising Ze'ev that his sister-in-law's cancer had completely disappeared and that she was healed. Six months of treatments had come to a positive resolution, and Mrs. Nanmoku stopped the absent healing on January 10, 1995, feeling perfectly fine again.

Can absent healing do as much as in-person treatments? Especially when there had been an in-person session, the results have been very good. Even when there was only absent healing, the results were positive. Bioenergetic force, like all energy, can travel great distances in a flash.

Dec. 2, 1994
To : Zeev Kolman

Dear Zeev,
MRS. NANMOKU'S CANCER has gone
and disappeared today. She is healed

   Delight,
   Relief,
   Rejoiceness,
   Thankfulness to you,
   Love to the God.

Please join her in sharing
her extreme happiness.

May God bless Zeev.

Toshimi Kawa

By now Ze'ev's reputation as an effective healer, as a source of alternative medical treatment, had become known in the United States as well as in Japan, Austria, Poland, and England. People in those countries sought him out or, in some cases, used absent healing. By now, too, Ze'ev understood his mission better: He was to do his bioenergetic work full time and on a professional basis, charging an appropriate fee just as medical people do, but also taking on cases without payment when the people coming to him could not afford to pay.

Prince Alfred von Liechtenstein, scion of a distinguished European family and president of the Vienna (Austria) International Academy for the Study of the Future, had met Ze'ev in 1989 and had recognized his extraordinary gift. The prince's treatments had given him a much higher energy level and had increased his general well-being. But it was a friend for whom the prince sought Ze'ev's help in a crisis, which added to his increasing success rate.

Ewai C., a busy real-estate executive living in San Francisco, had been wearing experimental extended-wear gas permeable contact lenses for approximately one year. The day before leaving for New York City, her eyes were tearing because of excruciating pain. Her vision became blurred and worsened as the day progressed. She was taken to the emergency eye clinic at Kaiser Hospital in San Francisco and was told by the ophthalmologist that her eyes were so badly damaged that she should not even consider wearing contact lenses again. She was advised not to travel, because of the risk of eye infection, but in any event to contact an ophthalmologist immediately on arrival in New York City for further treatment. Instead, Ewai met Ze'ev, who began treating her eyes. In the span of two weeks she received three treatments from him.

Upon her return to San Francisco, she went back to Kaiser Hospital and her local doctor. There was no evidence of scar tissue or any damage, the doctor informed her in amazement. Her eyes had completely healed. Upon further examination, the doctor discovered that somehow her vision had significantly and dramatically improved. He prescribed new, weaker glasses and contact lenses that she continues to wear to this day without any problems whatever. I also know Ewai and can attest that she has no eye problems of any kind now.

A couple originally from Japan, Mr. and Mrs. Taka Otsuka, sought Ze'ev in the fall of 1990. Mr. Otsuka had suffered from stomach trouble and pain, and despite careful medical examination the doctors could not diagnose the cause of his troubles. The first session with Ze'ev stopped the pain altogether; Mr. Otsuka's stomach area "turned very warm and digestion began to work" again. After several treatments, Mr. Otsuka was healed and is to this day. Mrs. Otsuka had suffered from arthritis in her hands and legs, a condition medical science really has no cure for at present. But Ze'ev's treatments stopped the pain, and it has not returned since.

In the middle of November 1993, Carol N. of New York was suffering from a medically diagnosed case of bleeding polyps of the lower stomach area and was due for an operation as soon as possible. But Carol N. had met Ze'ev and asked him to treat her. Without being told the nature of her problem, Ze'ev correctly diagnosed the situation and gave her a treatment. During this, Carol N. experienced a "kind of electric shock." Ze'ev informed her that the polyps were out of her body; liquid became apparent in the area where the polyps had been. Carol N. wiped off the liquid with a tissue.

When she returned to the hospital where the original diagnosis had been made and where she was due for surgery, the examining physician informed her that he could find no trace of the polyps, and he canceled the operation. This occurred on November 30, 1993, about two weeks after the original problem was diagnosed.

Boris Said is a professional documentary filmmaker living in New York. In February 1993, he suffered an accident in his apartment and sustained three broken ribs and damage to his lungs. A friend had heard of Ze'ev, who was then in New York City, and suggested a visit to him. Perhaps Mr. Said's own words will describe best what transpired next.

MAGICAL EYE
I N C O R P O R A T E D

5 February 1993

To Whom It May Concern:

I am a patient of Zeev Kolman. I heard about Zeev's abilities from a friend, Clarence Robins, of Queens, N.Y. after sustaining injuries in a fall in my New York City apartment on February 16, 1993.

I had broken three ribs (Nos. 7, 8 and 9 on the right side.) in a fall in my bathroom. On February 18 I was hospitalized at Beth Israel Hospital in New York when X-rays showed that my right lung had been punctured and had filled with blood. On the morning after the lung was drained, my doctor informed me that I would need open-chest surgery to remove excess dried blood from the inside of my right lung. The doctor warned me that I would permanently lose at least 60 per cent of the use of my right lung if I did not undergo surgery immediately. I had no insurance, and could not afford the estimated cost of $ 28,000.

The doctor also advised me that I would be laid up for at least 3 months. Such a lay-off would have cost me the loss of a film project on which I had been working for two years.

I visited Zeev Kolman three times during the two weeks following my release from hospital at 76 Madison Avenue, in New York City. After the first visit, I could no longer feel my ribs moving against each other when I breathed. After the second visit, most of the pain was gone, and by the end of the third visit, my breathing had returned to normal.

Recent X-rays confirm that my right lung is now 95 per cent effective. I resumed a full range of normal activity 6 weeks after my third and final visit to Zeev Kolman.

Zeev Kolman's extraordinary healing abilities are the only possible explanation for my amazing recovery. I am 60 years of age. My doctor tells me he is amazed at the speed with which my ribs knit together. He seems totally mystified about the present condition of my lung!

I have nothing but the highest admiration for Mr. Kolman and his amazing gift. My X-rays are graphic proof of his abilities, and are available to anyone who has doubts.

Signed:

Boris Said

Seemingly hopeless cases, medically speaking, are sometimes grist for Ze'ev's healing mills. Anita Gurevich's ten-year-old daughter, Yael, had profound hearing problems, diagnosed because of a series of tests that physicians at the Baltimore, Maryland, Ear, Nose & Throat Associates facility termed abnormal. After a series of Ze'ev's treatments, Yael's hearing became normal; the child has no further difficulties.

Perhaps one of Ze'ev's most interesting current cases concerns Irshad Ullah Khan, a respected businessman and world-renowned Pathan poet who had been suffering from a serious heart ailment, essentially a life-threatening condition. Mr. Ullah Khan underwent two serious operations, one a directional coronary atherectomy with angioplasty on January 6, 1993, and a second one (because of recurrent problems), intervention with a laser angioplasty, on June 30, 1993, at Massachusetts General Hospital in Boston. But both failed

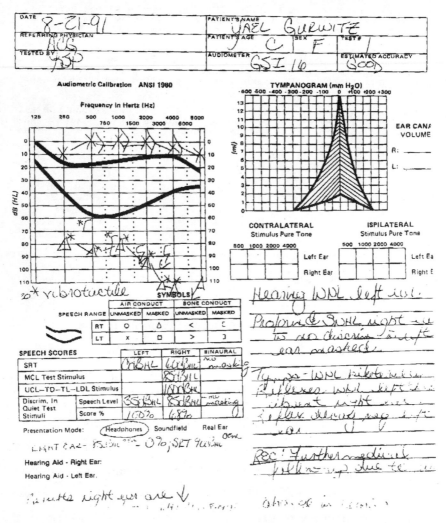

EAR, NOSE & THROAT ASSOCIATES

THE PHYSICIANS PAVILION • 6565 N. CHARLES STREET • SUITE 601 • BALTIMORE, MARYLAND 21204 • (301) 821-5151

GEORGE C. ALDERMAN, M.D., F.A.C.S.
SAMUEL M. M. LUMPKIN, M.D., F.A.C.S.

J. DENNIS BRANGER, M.D., F.A.C.S.
KARL W. DIEHN, M.D., F.A.C.S.
ANDREW C. GOLDSTONE, M.D.

AUDIOLOGICAL EVALUATION

REASON FOR REFERRAL | NAME OF REFERRING STATION

AIR CONDUCTION

EXAMINER'S INITIALS	RIGHT								LEFT								
	250	500	1000	1500	2000	3000	4000	6000	8000	250	500	1000	1500	2000	3000	4000	6000	8000
	65	75	70	70	75	75	80	90	80	10	10	5	10	10	10	5	30	35
MASKING LEVEL		100 / 50																

BONE CONDUCTION

EXAMINER'S INITIALS	RIGHT							LEFT						
	250	500	1000	1500	2000	3000	4000	250	500	1000	1500	2000	3000	4000
			75+											
MASKING LEVEL			80											

ACOUSTIC IMMITTANCE

	RESTING PRESSURE	PVT	STATIC MEASUREMENT	PROBE LEFT	RESTING PRESSURE	PVT	STATIC MEASUREMENT		EAR	TWO FREQ.	THREE FREQ.
PROBE RIGHT								RIGHT			

PURETONE AVERAGES

STIMULUS LEFT	CONTRALATERAL AR THRESHOLDS				REFLEX DECAY		STIMULUS RIGHT			LEFT		
	500	1000	2000	4000	500	1000		500	1000	2000	4000	500	1000

INTER-TEST CONSISTENCY

| | | | | | | | RIGHT | LEFT |

| STIMULUS RIGHT | IPSILATERAL AR THRESHOLDS | | HALF-LIFE | STIMULUS LEFT | IPSILATERAL AR THRESHOLDS | | HALF-LIFE | |

REMARKS: ® . abnormal   Ⓛ -- WNL

SPEECH AUDIOMETRY

EXAMINER'S INITIAL'S	SRT		RIGHT EAR DISCRIMINATION						LEFT EAR DISCRIMINATION					
	1	2	1	2	3	4	5	PBMAX	PI/PB	1	2	3	4	5	PBMAX	PI/PB
RIGHT EAR		%	100% 0%							% 100%				
LEFT EAR		HL	90 90 70							HL 50				
MASKING LEVEL														

COMMENTS:

Pt. hx Tag ... He neg
neg F, H, 7 yrs ago cerumen ...
canal now clear -- ...
3-6 mos ago began c/o ...

® SDT 70 , 100/50 dB; NR 100/100 db
90 dB "soft" 95 dB "medium" 100 dB
cerumeasses bilat
cones of lot ...
c/o + ac... gradua
onset initially, ...

LAST NAME - FIRST NAME - MIDDLE INITIAL: GURWITZ, YAEL   AGE 10   CLASS ... SOCIAL SECURITY NO.

SIGNATURE OF EXAMINING AUDIOLOGIST: [signature]   DATE OF EXAM 8-19-91

AUDIOLOGICAL EVALUATIO

to relieve the heart condition, and it became clear that something drastic had to be done. Only with the constant use of nitroglycerine was Mr. Ullah Khan able to walk and continue his activities. Under the circumstances, his medical advisors decided on a heart bypass operation as the only way out, a risky one to be sure.

Mr. Ullah Khan was already scheduled for such surgery at the New York Hospital, Cornell Medical Center, when a friend told him of Ze'ev. After an initial consultation, which already afforded him immediate relief of his symptoms, Mr. Ullah Khan decided to postpone the operation to see if Ze'ev could actually help his condition in a serious and lasting way. Ze'ev then started an immediate series of intensive treatments, one after another, and it became clear that something was indeed happening. As a result, the operation was canceled because it was no longer necessary. Appropriate medical tests were instituted to make sure that the results of Ze'ev's treatments were indeed yielding these positive results. Dr. Jeffrey Borer of the Cornell Medical Center compared Mr. Ullah Khan's condition after the treatments to "a miracle."

Mr. Ullah Khan then went for a cardiovascular follow-up at Mount Sinai Medical Center. In his report to Dr. Harvey Klein of Cornell, Dr. Valentin Fuster of Mount Sinai indicated that "a gated exercise test, just performed at New York Hospital, did not reveal ventricular dysfunction on exercise."

This report would not have been possible prior to Ze'ev's treatments.

Mr. Ullah Khan, whom I have met several times, has been well ever since and has long resumed his normal life and full business activities without any problems whatever.

If anything, this case proves that careful consultation with medical experts to determine the problem, but not necessarily following all suggestions as to treatments, can indeed benefit the patient. When I spoke to Dr. Klein, he was most enthusiastic about the results of Ze'ev's treatments and the idea of cooperation between traditional medicine and alternative paths, so well documented by this case.

BORER
922282

NYH Hosp ID : 235-81-96
Age,Gender : 49 yrs Male

THE NEW YORK HOSPITAL - CORNELL MEDICAL CENTER
CARDIAC CATHETERIZATION LABORATORY
FINAL REPORT
525 EAST 68th St,STARR 446, NY,NY 10021 Tel:(212)746-4644 Fax:(212)746-8295

INDICATIONS FOR CATHETERIZATION
Angina Class-II

PROCEDURES
Left heart catheterization
Coronary angiography
Left ventriculogram

HEMODYNAMICS HR: 80 Rhythm: SINUS BSA:1.94 m2
Chamber   Pressure(mmHg)(mean)   O2 Sat(%)
LV   116/12
AORTA   116/80 [98]

CORONARY ANGIOGRAPHY Dominance: RIGHT
LEFT MAIN
        ..... Normal
LAD   (large vessel)
   Prox ..... 50% stenosis INVOLVING FIRST SEPTAL
   Mid   ..... 80% stenosis ECCENTRIC, COMPLEX
             LESION INVOLVING SECOND SEPTAL
CIRCUMFLEX (large vessel)
        ..... Normal
RCA   (large vessel)
        ..... Normal

VALVULAR FUNCTION
MITRAL
   Prolapse   NONE
   Regurgitation   NONE

LEFT VENTRICULOGRAM
COMMENTS
1. EF ~ 58%

CONCLUSIONS
1. Normal global left ventricular function, ejection fraction of 58%
2. Single-vessel coronary artery disease

Geoffrey Bergman, MD
Associate Director
Cardiac Catheterization Laboratory

Anthony Inguaggiato, MD
Asst. Attending Physician
Cardiac Catheterization Laboratory

THE NEW YORK HOSPITAL-CORNELL MEDICAL CENTER

NUCLEAR CARDIOLOGY LABORATORY

TEST: Radionuclide Cineangiogram

[x] Equilibrium Technique
[ ] First Pass Technique
[ ] Gated Tc99m Sestamibi Technique

PRESUMPTIVE DIAGNOSIS:
S/P atherectomy

	Heart Rate	Arterial Pressure	Ejection Fraction Left Ventricle	Right Ventricle
Rest	81	130/86	63% (nl. = 45 — 75%)	(nl. = 40 — 65%)
Exercise	125	156/90	57% (nl. = >55%)	(nl. = >45%)
Intervention				
Intervention				
Intervention				

(Note: In normal subjects, right and left ventricular ejection fractions usually rise > 5% during exercise compared with values at rest.)

DURATION OF EXERCISE: 7 minutes 30 seconds   MAXIMAL EXERCISE LOAD: 75 Watts
REASON FOR CESSATION OF EXERCISE: Increasing Chest Discomfort

INTERPRETATION OF IMAGE DISPLAY AND CONCLUSIONS:

In the LAO position at rest there is normal global function. During maximal exercise, septal and apical hypokinesis develops.

CONCLUSIONS:

The magnitude of decrease of the LVEF response to maximal exercise indicates the presence of functionally mild to moderate ischemia at the present time.

DAVID V. BECKER, M.D.

DIVISION OF NUCLEAR MEDICINE
DEPARTMENT OF RADIOLOGY

MICHAEL ZUKOWSKY, M.D.
JEFFREY S. BORER, M.D.

DIVISION OF CARDIOLOGY
DEPARTMENT OF MEDICINE

THE NEW YORK HOSPITAL-CORNELL MEDICAL CENTER

NUCLEAR CARDIOLOGY LABORATORY

TEST: Radionuclide Cineangiogram

[x] Equilibrium Technique
[ ] First Pass Technique
[ ] Gated Tc99m Sestamibi Technique

PRESUMPTIVE DIAGNOSIS:
CAD

	Heart Rate	Arterial Pressure	Ejection Fraction Left Ventricle	Right Ventricle
Rest	64	94/60	(nl. = 45 — 75%) 58%	(nl. = 40 — 65%)
Exercise	118	130/82	(nl. = >55%) 52%	(nl. = >45%)
Intervention				
Intervention				
Intervention				

(Note: In normal subjects, right and left ventricular ejection fractions usually rise > 5% during exercise compared with values at rest.)

DURATION OF EXERCISE: 8 2/3 minutes   MAXIMAL EXERCISE LOAD: 85 Watts
REASON FOR CESSATION OF EXERCISE: Chest pain and fatigue

INTERPRETATION OF IMAGE DISPLAY AND CONCLUSIONS:

With the patient at rest in the left anterior oblique position, global and regional left ventricular function wa normal. During exercise, global left ventricular function decreased due to the development of septal and apical hypokinesia. The magnitude of the decrease in left ventricular function from rest to exercise is consistent with functionally mild to moderate left ventricular ischemia.

DAVID V. BECKER, M.D.

EDMUND HERROLD, M.D.
JEFFREY S. BORER, M.D.

The Mount Sinai Medical Center

The Mount Sinai Hospital
Mount Sinai School of Medicine

One Gustave L. Levy Place
New York. NY 10029—6574

Valentin Fuster, M.D., Ph.D.
Arthur M. & Hilda A. Master
Professor of Medicine
Director Cardiovascular Institute

Box 1080

Tel (212) 241-7911
Fax (212) 423-9488

February 24, 1994

Harvey Klein, M.D.
The New York Hospital
Cornell University Medical Center
525 East 68th Street, Starr 1
New York, NY 10021

Re: Mr. Irshad Ullah Khan, Age 49

Dear Dr. Klein:

I had the pleasure to see Mr. Ullah Khan today for cardiovascular follow up. In brief,
as you know, Mr. Ullah Khan underwent directional coronary atherectomy on 1/6/93
and because of recurrent stenosis he underwent laser angioplasty on 6/30/93. I have
the following comments:

1.   A number of weeks ago, Mr. Khan had atypical pain which was unpredictable
       and, therefore, probably there was a component of vasospasm. Non
       conventional therapy by an Israeli therapist has certainly improved Mr. Khan
       significantly from the point of view of his psychological status and from the fact
       that he does not have any more angina despite walking five miles a day at a
       reasonable speed.

2.   However, I was concerned since, in my experience, the above therapy does
       not have an effect on the coronary anatomy. Therefore, I urged
       Mr. Ullah Khan to have a treadmill exercise test with Thallium perfusion
       imaging. As originally, the electrocardiogram was equivocal (about 1mm ST
       depression) but Thallium perfusion imaging revealed moderate to severe
       anteroseptal apical and infero-posterior ischemia. For the record, blood
       pressure response during exercise was normal and Mr. Ullah Khan exercised
       for about 13 minutes.

3.   According to the above information, I indicated to Mr. Ullah Khan the following:
       a) That his coronary artery disease is not severe, basically proximal LAD
       stenosis also with severe disease in the diagonal branches .

February 24, 1994
Harvey Klein, M.D.
Page 2

b) Mr. Khan has to realize that he does not have the warning symptoms of angina and, therefore, we have to come to a conclusion of how much he can do and whether or not an interventional procedure should be undertaken.

c) Within the context of a conservative approach, I asked Mr. Ullah Khan to check his heart rate after his five mile walk, then I will repeat an exercise study with a gated mode that I will compare with our previous results. If there is not much significant ventricular dysfunction, I will treat Mr. Ullah Khan conservatively. If there is significant ventricular dysfunction, we should consider bypass surgery with an internal mammary artery.

We will be in touch.

Sincerely,

Valentin Fuster, M.D., Ph.D.
VF:cme

cc: Mr. Ullah Khan

P.D.   A gated exercise test, just performed at New York Hospital, did not reveal ventricular dysfunction on exercise. Ejection fraction at rest was 53%, after 12 minutes (75 watts) it was 78% (better than prior to PTCA). I will take conservative approach.

This proves the effectiveness of Ze'ev Kolman's treatment IUK

Michael Solter is an Israeli-born businessman who has lived in New York for some time. In 1992, his mother-in-law, Hannah Rubin, age 67, was struck by a car. An ambulance removed her to Boot Memorial Hospital in Flushing, New York. For a month and a half she was given intensive care, but she remained in a deep coma and on life-support machines for four months. The medical prognosis was not good for her ever regaining consciousness, and the doctors advised that perhaps it would be best to remove the life-support equipment and let her pass on.

It was at that moment that destiny took a hand. At a gathering, Mr. Solter met a man who was sympathetic to Mrs. Rubin's plight, and he suggested that there was, perhaps, a way to try and save her life. He had heard of Ze'ev, and Mr. Solter eagerly made the contact. The doctors at the hospital would not hear of such treatment. But Ze'ev went there, anyway, quietly, and gave her a treatment. Immediately thereafter, she opened her eyes—for the first time since the accident.

"I'll be back the end of the week," a determined Ze'ev told Mr. Solter.

The second treatment had even more startling results. As Ze'ev passed his hands over Mrs. Rubin, projecting energy, the equipment giving her life support began to act on its own, moving, rattling as if struck by electric power!

That night Mrs. Rubin started to speak again. Within days she was her old self. Today, more than three years later, she is well, and no sign of the accident has remained.

Sometimes I wonder about the mentality of medical professionals, especially those with moribund patients on their hands. One would think that a healer with an established track record of successful healings ought to be welcomed by doctors to try and help when they cannot do so. Instead, many medical people view all nonconventional healers as the competition.

Even in far-off Poland, Ze'ev's reputation caused an urgent request for help. The chief rabbi of Poland and of the city of Lodz had been suffering from a severe heart condition, causing him much chest pain. After three treatments from Ze'ev he had no pains at all, according to his rather flowery statement of gratitude sent via his Brooklyn, New York, representative.

Back in Israel, where he still worked part time, Ze'ev became the subject of interviews and much curiosity. The reputable newspaper *Yedioth Ahronot* wrote of Ze'ev in its May 15, 1992, edition: "Paralyzed people began to walk, the deaf could hear again, skin-diseased people were healed, migraine headache sufferers got rid of their headaches permanently, and cancer patients were healed as well."

While Ze'ev's successful cases increased, people in the scientific community emerged, wondering what it was that he had with which to do this work. Unfortunately, most of these sincere (but otherwise unknowing) scientists approached Ze'ev as if he were a laboratory animal to be outfitted with wires connected to instruments in the forlorn hope of discovering the "magical" powers that allow him to do his work. There is nothing supernatural or religious involved in Ze'ev's healing (except his personal faith). Bioenergy, the natural life force in all of us, is the source.

PART THREE

15

Self-Healing

To be sure, Ze'ev cannot turn you into a healer by telling you how he does it or how it works. Bioenergetic healing is a gift few individuals possess, some more than others, and you can't take it in school like Healing 101.

But one of the cornerstones of Ze'ev's approach to bioenergetic healing is the need to continue what he has started either in person or by absent healing on the telephone. Patients can continue the beneficial effects of Ze'ev's ministrations after their sessions are over by following a simple set of rules and exercises. In his workshops that is precisely what he teaches to people eager to learn how to relax and to heal themselves in body, mind, and spirit.

For about ten minutes, at the outset, students undergo deep meditation exercises, not unlike yoga meditation, for much the same purposes. Soothing music is played in the background, selected from tapes available for precisely this purpose. In his workshops, Ze'ev determines how long this phase should take; when you do it, your body will indicate when it is the right moment to discontinue this phase and to move on to the next.

Follow your meditation with a breathing exercise, because your body requires more oxygen than normal breathing supplies, according to Ze'ev. But prior to replenishing your body with fresh oxygen, Ze'ev suggests that you remove the used-up, bad air by visualizing it and then removing it by breathing it out through your mouth. This is followed by deep breathing to replenish the used-up air with fresh oxygen. Breathe out through your nose and make a kind of hissing sound to strengthen the action and results.

Ze'ev suggests that you take several groups of three deep breaths, each breath held long and then expelled. Direct each group of breaths toward a different part of your body: feet, hands, stomach area, and head and brain. Close your eyes and visualize the oxygen reaching out to and arriving at the various parts of your body. Breathe in through your nose and out through your mouth unhurriedly while you are deeply relaxed. Hold each breath for as long as is comfortable.

With fresh oxygen comes the energy. Through visualization the energy is carefully "sent," that is, directed, to parts of your body while you take particular care to touch on each important part.

Next, sit again in meditation with your hands extended palms up to receive energy, the chakra of your head and forehead (upper solar plexus) followed by the chakras of your hands opening to receive this force. (Whether one refers to these focal points by the traditional Indian terminology, or by Chinese terms, or by Western nomenclature is immaterial—they all refer to centers in the body where biological energy can be absorbed most readily.)

Sit like this for about ten minutes; gradually, you may feel "needles" touching the palms of your hands. This is a sign that your body is receiving energy. By holding up your hands with palms facing each other twenty or twenty-five inches apart, you will feel energy flowing from palm to palm, proof that this force has indeed been raised. Apply this energy to yourself or to another person. Applying it to yourself does not cause any kind of short-circuit as you may expect, but it has stronger effects than if you apply it to another person.

Ze'ev maintains that in self-healing, energy drawn from external power sources combines with the person's own energy to effect healing; if it were only the person's own energy potential, no improvement would result. What, then, are the sources for this external energy? Radiation from the sun, moon, and planets sends continuous streams of particles in the form of cosmic radiation. These particles bombard us and cause certain subtle changes in our bodies, both at the time of birth when we first are touched by them and throughout our lives. Cosmic radiation, then, coming only from our solar system is the physical basis for astrology's claims regarding influences from "the stars," except that astrologers know very well that the stars are far too distant to exercise any strong influence. It is the planets, the sun, and the moon that send the strongest radiation to earth and to us.

The purpose of these exercises is primarily self-healing and not an attempt to turn students into incipient healers. On occasion, when there was no other way, Ze'ev has given energy to a person who then transmits it to an ailing person at another location. However, he cautions that this should be done only for five minutes—doing it any longer would tend to deplete the person transmitting the energy and cause the person sending the energy to feel exhausted and also lacking in energy.

Ze'ev also teaches his students and the public how to construct a defense layer around themselves which he calls the Blue Shield. In parapsychology, this is sometimes referred to as psychic self-defense. First, close your eyes and imagine yourself, your appearance, in the negative, like a photographic negative. Next, see in your mind's eye light surrounding yourself. This light can be white, blue, or purple, but it must be of a light shade. Now open your eyes again. With your hands, describe the outline of a protective shield that follows your body contours. According to Ze'ev, the aura consists of several layers, and this shield protects them all. The purpose of the shield is to protect you from the emanations from others, which may or may not be negative or dangerous. It is Ze'ev's contention that energy goes forth from all of us all the time and affects others in various ways. What he calls "energies" are what the public often refers to as "vibrations," and sensitive people know how real these emanations can be. Ze'ev feels that the majority of these energies are sent on purpose and are not something over which the sender has no control.

What it boils down to is this: Self-healing, as Ze'ev understands it, refers to an overall improvement of one's condition—physical, mental, and spiritual. This is achieved through the exercises described: meditation, breathing exercises, including removing "bad" energies, and directing energy to various parts of the body.

If you are ill when you use these exercises, chances are they will lessen the pain and discomfort. But Ze'ev emphasizes that they are not a substitute for his healing sessions in person or via absent healing. He cannot transfer his unique powers of healing to people by having them perform certain exercises, no matter how beneficial they are.

Nor does Ze'ev intend to conduct courses in the development of healing powers to make people into healers. However, if a truly gifted healer comes along who can demonstrate ability through actual work, Ze'ev will always lend a hand to develop and guide such a gifted person further along the way. There can never be enough bioenergetic healers to deal with the many who truly need their services.

16

Locating Missing Persons

It is not unusual for gifted psychic individuals to have paranormal abilities in more than one area, even though they stress the aspect that seems strongest for them. Ze'ev is a psychically active person, but his bioenergetic healing work is his main gift and he rightfully stresses this aspect.

Nevertheless, he was from the outset aware of other psychic abilities, such as the locating of missing persons, dead or alive, through a kind of traveling clairvoyance involving a state of light trance. This state is markedly different from true, deep trance, during which there occurs what is called in parapsychology "dissociation of personality." Another entity frequently takes over the body of the medium and communicates directly with the questioner, using only the physical apparatus of the entranced medium as a communication tool and not involving the medium's personality in any way, conscious or unconscious.

Today, Ze'ev hesitates to use that part of his gift except in truly extraordinary circumstances, concentrating his energies instead on his healing work. Nevertheless, his track record of locating missing persons is remarkable. He has also long come to terms with that aspect of his abilities, so long as it does not diminish his work as a healer.

The opening of the energy channels to the spiritual also brought about certain abilities over a wide range of psychic phenomena. Together with the gift of healing I was granted in the Sinai Desert, there were other things that happened to me, such as the seeing of auras, entities, telepathy, and the location of missing persons.

All this began during one of my stints of reserve duty in 1977. At first, when we traveled in armored carriers in the desert, I would visualize, to amuse myself, what things would look like beyond the next ridge, and what I had "imagined" turned out absolutely accurate. The soldiers of my unit regarded me as having parapsychological powers, even though I myself was not convinced that this was so.

Our reserve duty that year was at Eilat on the Red Sea. On a particular morning, at about 10:00 A.M., I lay stretched out on the beach, my face on a towel, allowing my back to tan in the summer sun. As I lay in the sweltering heat, I suddenly felt a tap on my shoulder and an unfamiliar voice asked me, "Are you Ze'ev Kolman?" Surprised, I turned my head, and before me stood an army officer whom I did not recognize. "I heard that you have parapsychological powers," he said. "Can you help us?"

It appeared that two soldiers had left for the desert in a jeep. One of them was found unconscious, lying at the side of the road without the other. The name of the missing soldier was Asher Peri, and I was now being asked to help in the search for him. I agreed to try to see what I could do. When we set out, we were told that the search area began near the great Mushroom Rock at the foot of King Solomon's Pillars. We drove on what seemed to be an endless road. I sat deep in thought at the right window, and to my left, in the middle seat, sat another officer. Suddenly, I went into trance and pictures began appearing before my eyes. I saw a cliff and a cave near it. Asher entered the cave, rested in its shade for awhile, and then I saw him walking on a high plateau and suddenly collapsing and falling into an abyss, losing consciousness, and dying. I saw his body lying there. Earth had fallen after him and covered part of his body; his army boots remained shining and highly visible. A few days later, the body was found in the exact place I had described, in the exact condition and position I had seen in the vision.

In the following years, I aided the police and security forces in the location of missing persons, soldiers and civilians as well. One night I was rudely awakened by the ringing of the telephone. A man wanted to talk to me. He had received my number from a mutual friend. He told me he was in urgent need of my assistance; he had just arrived in Israel from the United States, and he was a professor of science at the Weizmann Institute in Rehovot. Then he asked me if I had heard of a young woman named Dafi Spiegel, of Ness Ziona, who had disappeared without a trace. I had indeed read about the case.

I suggested we meet the following morning. As I sat with the phone in my hand, I suddenly told the professor I saw the young woman psychically. She was no longer alive, and her body was in an orchard on the border of the city of Rehovot, close to the railroad track that separated Rehovot and Ness Ziona. I described a house marked "3a" and next to it a solitary pine tree close to a wire fence. The other end of the line became deathly silent. I kept talking and described a gray and white poodle and the picture of a young woman lying on her back, in a bathing suit, but I added that this picture was not related to her death. The pictures kept flashing by like a movie. I described Dafi as she appeared to me: her age, her height, the color of her eyes, and a long braid of hair falling from her head.

The professor asked my permission to bring me to the home of Dafi Spiegel's parents. I repeated that it was late at night, but he insisted I come.

Fifteen minutes later he arrived at my home in Holon, and we drove to the Spiegel family home in Ness Ziona. He explained that his daughter was the closest friend of the missing Dafi Spiegel. We were now supposed to turn on the road that led to the city proper, but to my amazement the car continued on the highway, passing by the side of the city and continuing in the direction of Rehovot. The professor seemed to be peering intently into the darkness, and his eyes blinked. I realized at once that he was driving in a trance and decided to let him drive wherever the steering wheel led him. Then suddenly, on the way to Rehovot, between the orchards the car slowed down, and the driver turned right and entered the orchard. I looked at him, each of us in a state of light trance. I knew that the direction in which he was driving was correct.

As we drove along slowly, we came upon a fork where we could veer right or left. After long moments of silence, the professor turned to me. "Where should we turn? Right or left?" "Turn wherever the wheel leads you," I replied. We turned left, and after a short drive we came across a building that had the number 3a on it. We got out of the car, and before us stood a solitary pine tree.

As I looked at the tree, I sensed that this was where the body lay. The professor walked toward the building and suddenly cried out in the dark, "Here is the wire fence you described!" I said, "Let's go back. We dare not enter this place, and we don't know who is there. Tomorrow morning you will bring help and check it out!" We finally drove back to the highway and turned left toward Ness Ziona. We entered the house of the Spiegel family. Suddenly I saw a photograph of Dafi lying on her back in a bathing suit! I did not tell the family anything about our trip to the orchard. We left with heavy hearts.

During the trip I saw a picture of Dafi with her eyes vacant, and to me that was an indication she was dead. The next morning a group went out to search for Dafi in the building inside the orchard I had indicated, which turned out to be a packing shed for oranges. In spite of the searches, nothing was found in the vicinity; the search continued the next day, but in vain.

That night, once again I went into trance and suddenly saw myself at the corner of Ahad Ha'am and Bar Ilan streets in Tel Aviv, looking north in the direction of the Habimah Theater. Before me I saw Dafi Spiegel standing at the corner, dressed in a tricot shirt, with her long braid over her shoulder, looking toward a gray building across the road, standing and staring at it as if surprised and expectant. I saw a clock, and before my eyes it moved from noon to 1:00 P.M., 2:00 P.M., and so on. At 5:00 P.M. I saw a young man leaving the building and coming toward her. It appeared as if there was an argument between them. He left, but she remained in place.

I came out of trance and looked at the people around me. The professor was shocked. "On that street, in that building lives Dafi's boyfriend," he said. The search for Dafi continued the next day. In the end her body was found in the orchard, near the tree, a few hundred yards further on in the orchard, not far from the building labeled "3a." At the inquest it was ruled that Dafi had put an end to her own life with a revolver her father kept hidden at home. I felt that Dafi had remained alone in the packing shed, where she had left her imprint, her misery, and her loneliness—and that was why my feelings were so strong about it.

The search for missing people and finding where they met their death has always left me drained and depressed. In spite of my gift in this area, I prefer dealing with bioenergy, and only in exceptional circumstances do I become involved in cases of this kind.

True, but then what is exceptional? Ze'ev is a very feeling man, and a plea for help when all else has failed is rarely ignored. To be sure, he isn't about to help you find your lost cat. Cases that have baffled police when there is suspicion of foul play, especially when he is able to pick up a lead immediately after being contacted— those are instances when Ze'ev will lend his considerable talent of locating missing persons. But he definitely is not in the lost-and-found business. Still, when he does become involved in such cases, there are nearly always positive results.

In 1990, already spending part of his time in New York City, Ze'ev was contacted by the wife of an aged Brooklyn rabbi who was missing. Ze'ev went into his peculiar brand of light trance and imme-diately asserted that the rabbi was no longer alive in the physical world. He described a junkyard near water and a street sign reading "61st Street." There, Ze'ev said, the body would be located. The police followed the lead and failed to find the body. But three days later the body was discovered at water's edge, near 61st Street in Brooklyn.

Joseph Lavi, who has become Ze'ev's friend, is sometimes con-tacted by people who want Ze'ev to help them in such cases. So it happened that during the Jewish holidays of 1992, Ze'ev was with his family in Israel when Mr. Lavi received a call from his former partner, Bruno, who lived in New Jersey. This was the night of Yom Kippur, the most sacred Jewish holy day. Bruno's neighbor, a successful lawyer and the father of two children, had failed to return home for the holiday. This seemed totally out of character for the man, who observed religious holidays meticulously. Under the circumstances, Bruno asked Mr. Lavi to call upon Ze'ev.

The family contacted Ze'ev by telephone in Israel, and Ze'ev offered to help. In a semitrance state he described a vision involving a large bridge, and on the bridge he noticed a suitcase. He even described its contents: a yarmulke (a small skullcap worn by religious Jews) and a wedding ring. He then spoke of a young man on that bridge jumping into the water and described the wedding ring as being composed of three colors of gold, which is rather unusual for a wedding ring.

Naturally, the family was upset at this news: a religious man committing suicide and on Yom Kippur? Clearly, this man from Israel was a fake! Just the same, the family placed a second call to Ze'ev the day after Yom Kippur, and this time he described the place where the body would be found. There would be bushes covering it, and an old white abandoned truck would be on the shore nearby. The body would be found three miles from shore. Thanks to some good connections, the family was able to get the police to bring scuba divers to look where Ze'ev had indicated the body was, but after several hours of not finding it, they gave up the search.

The police demanded some kind of evidence that the man from Israel was telling the truth. A conference call was arranged among the family, the police, and Ze'ev.

"There will be a helicopter flying over the spot shortly," Ze'ev told the incredulous police. "It will be white with red markings, and that is the exact spot where you must look for the body."

In exactly two minutes such a helicopter appeared overhead, marking the spot. How could Ze'ev have known this thousands of miles away? Once again the police looked, and this time they discovered the body where Ze'ev had indicated.

Why did the police not find it earlier? Because the tide had since changed from high to low, and it was only at low tide that the body became visible in the water. Everything was exactly as Ze'ev had described it: the bushes hiding the body, the white truck abandoned on the beach.

But how could the lawyer have left the house and reached the bridge when his car was not missing? the family wanted to know. Once again Ze'ev invoked his clairvoyant powers. He described the young man walking out of the house and "saw" him walking to the bus station. But the family said, Impossible, there is no way to get through because the only road is a dead-end street. "He took a shortcut," Ze'ev insisted. The family knew of no shortcut, but upon checking they found a shortcut all right, though the family had never used it.

In parapsychology we call this gift "traveling clairvoyance," and it is rare indeed, especially to the extent Ze'ev has it.

But not every case is as sad as this one. A young girl had disappeared from her family's home in Brooklyn, and the family turned to Ze'ev, whom they knew, for help. In his light trance, Ze'ev described the girl as being lost in the Connecticut woods, but alive and well. Police and the FBI had failed to find her, yet the following day she was indeed discovered alive and well in the Connecticut woods.

The question, especially in cases when the missing person is already dead, is, What exactly allows Ze'ev to do this work and to do it so accurately? Certainly, his native clairvoyant ability is the tool that enables him to reach out at a distance and to "see" what transpired. But there are cases involving other psychics when the angry spirit of the victim of foul play guides the psychic to where its body is. Ze'ev is not generally aware of spirit assistance, but he does credit his guides in an overall sense with the success of this phase of his work.

17

The Wider World
of Kolman the Healer

The people who come to Ze'ev do so because of word of mouth, because a friend told them, and occasionally even on the advice of a progressive medical doctor who cannot provide a cure by conventional means. Occasionally, a magazine or newspaper story will catch the attention of a reader in need of help, but true healers neither advertise nor guarantee results; they serve, as and when called upon.

People in all walks of life seek out Ze'ev. Celebrities, for a variety of reasons, have reached out to him: Melanie Griffith, Don Johnson, Barbra Streisand, John Denver, Raquel Welch, Carly Simon, Goldie Hawn, and Robert Wagner of the entertainment world. Senator Claiborne Pell has benefited from a treatment.

Medical people who are familiar with Ze'ev's work, such as Dr. Enrique J. Teuscher, have this to say about him:

Ze'ev Kolman is an extraordinary bioenergist who uses non-contact therapeutic touch. His therapeutic effectiveness is quite broad. A girl deaf since birth regained about 75 percent of her hearing ability after treatment. Patients with terminal cancer conditions with two to three weeks to live according to their classical prognosis are doing well three to four years later. Ze'ev has successfully treated chronic pain syndromes and caused recession of tumors. After Ze'ev's treatments, arthritic deformities persist, but the patient can now move joints painlessly. After one treatment of ruptured lumbar discs causing severe sciatica and partial paralysis, a patient Ze'ev treated was able to get up with perceived full strength and without pain.

> Enrique J. Teuscher, M.D.
> Practicing psychiatrist and neurologist
> New Rochelle, New York

Harold C. Whitcomb, M.D., is an internist currently on the hospital board in Aspen, Colorado, and has been there since 1962. He is a widely respected doctor with many important papers to his credit. Because of his interest in bioenergetic medicine, he became acquainted with Ze'ev in February 1991 as a result of one of his patient's experiences with Ze'ev. The doctor himself experienced Ze'ev's therapy, and he stated: "I was truly impressed and subsequently referred a number of patients to Mr. Kolman, and the majority of them benefited significantly. His treatment is remarkably safe and very unusual. He is able to shift blocked energy which contributes to certain types of illness—and enables the patient to further progress in the healing process."

Victor Penzer, M.D., with doctorates from both Innsbruck and Munich universities, affiliated at various times with Mount Sinai and Beth Israel/Boston hospitals, on the faculty of Tufts and Boston universities, currently professor at the California Institute for Human Science, and a renowned medical researcher and international lecturer, met Ze'ev during one of his lecture tours. He said, "In April of 1985, I met not only Mr. Kolman, but also with several doctors who in difficult cases came to rely on Mr. Kolman's collaboration. From then on, I have met with Mr. Kolman several times. His gift is extraordinary and his skill in therapeutic application of Bioenergy is remarkable."

Paul N. Temple, chairman of the Institute of Noetic Sciences founded by former astronaut Edgar Mitchell, is familiar with Ze'ev's work and reputation: "I consider his original contributions to be of major significance to the healing arts in supplementing traditional medical and surgical procedures."

"An exceptionally gifted and loving person devoted to healing the body, mind, and soul," wrote the artist Carly Simon about her experiences with Ze'ev.

Ze'ev is always willing to cooperate with open-minded medical doctors or institutions, if the joint effort will benefit patients or genuine research accepting bioenergy as an important healing factor. As his work progresses and becomes better known internationally, he hopes a bioenergetic institute will emerge, properly supported and funded, to serve as a center for his work and associated subjects in the field of paranormal research. Interest in Ze'ev's work by organizations in the field of alternative medicine is considerable, because no healer of his stature has come along since Cayce. But rather than

Claiborne Pell
United States Senator
Washington, D.C. 20510

October 4, 1993

Dear Dr. Holzer:

Thank you for your letter of September 24, 1993 concerning Ke'ev Kolman.

I can say that he gave me a treatment and I did feel the warmth and healing power that was in his hands as he ran them closer by me.

You are quite right, too, in that I remain very interested in parapsychology and the progress of respectable alternative medicine.

Please use this letter if it would be helpful to you.

With every good wish, I am

Ever sincerely,

Claiborne Pell

Professor Hans Holzer, Ph.D.
140 Riverside Drive
New York, New York 10024-2605

use precious time and energies in furthering the research of many, a central institute, Ze'ev believes, will serve the cause of bioenergetic medicine best.

Ze'ev's principal interest and occupation these days is simply to help those needing healing. He conducts seminars and workshops now and again, in which he teaches the art of self-healing, valuable to people who do not seek out his services. Time and energy are his stock in trade, consequently he is wise not to use them in unsuitable pursuits such as purely social occasions or symposia looking into the basis of healing. He already knows what works, and social occasions, charity affairs, and the like are of interest primarily if they serve a cause he may be interested in or affiliated with—such as the quest for an institute.

People with minor ailments may find it more difficult to obtain appointments than those truly in urgent need of help for major causes, especially when conventional medicine has not helped. And as more and more medical doctors recognize the value of using both traditional and alternative methods of healing, appointments may become more scarce.

Ze'ev works in his Israel clinic and from time to time visits New York City.

Dear Hans:

I have known Ze'ev Kolman for several years and I am very much impressed with his abilities as a healer and as a person. All my experiences with him have been absolutely positive - and I am so happy to have him in my life.

Those who want to contact Mr. Kolman may do so by writing to him care of Beyond Words Publishing, Inc., 4443 NE Airport Road, Hillsboro, Oregon 97124-6074. Please enclose a self-addressed, stamped envelope. Do not telephone.

Biographical Notes

Ze'ev Kolman grew up in Holon, near Tel Aviv, Israel, fully intent on pursuing a career in his family's interior-decorating business. However, during a stint in the army, Ze'ev had an encounter that forever changed the course of his life. Gradually, he realized he had acquired great healing powers as a result of that encounter, and he now devotes himself entirely to the art of healing. His form of healing is called bioenergetics.

Ze'ev lives and works in Israel, where his family lives, and travels abroad, including the United States, when the need arises. Miriam, his wife, is a teacher; his son, Noam, 24, is in the construction field; his son, Evan, 22, is at Tel Aviv University studying business administration; and his daughter, Einat, 18, is serving her stint in the army.

Hans Holzer, Ph.D., is the author of more than one hundred books, many on psychical research subjects, including *Healing*

Beyond Medicine: Alternative Paths to Wellness, Life Beyond, and *The Directory of Psychics.* Prof. Holzer taught parapsychology for part of eight years at the New York Institute of Technology, lectures widely, and has been active in television and films as a writer-producer and host.

Prof. Holzer studied at Columbia University and the University of Vienna in Austria, and he received a Ph.D. from the London College of Applied Science. He is listed in *Who's Who in America* and lives in New York City.

BEYOND WORDS PUBLISHING, INC.

Our corporate mission

INSPIRE TO INTEGRITY

Our declared values

We give to all of life as life has given us.
We honor all relationships.
Trust and stewardship are integral
to fulfilling dreams.
Collaboration is essential to create miracles.
Creativity and aesthetics nourish the soul.
Unlimited thinking is fundamental.
Living your passion is vital.
Joy and humor open our hearts to growth.
It is important to remind ourselves of love.

Our promise to our customers

We will provide you with the highest quality books
and related products that meet or exceed your
expectations. As our customer, you will be satisfied
with your purchase and will receive your order
promptly, or we will refund your money.

OTHER BOOKS FROM
BEYOND WORDS PUBLISHING, INC.

YOU CAN HAVE IT ALL

Author: Arnold M. Patent, $16.95 hardcover

Joy, peace, abundance—these gifts of the Universe are available to each of us whenever we choose to play the *real* game of life: the game of mutual support. *You Can Have It All* is a guidebook that shows us how to move beyond our beliefs in struggle and shortage, open our hearts, and enjoy a life of true ecstasy. Arnold Patent first self-published *You Can Have It All* in 1984, and it became a classic with over 200,000 copies in print. This revised and expanded edition reflects his greater understanding of the principles and offers practical suggestions as well as simple exercises for improving the quality of our lives.

THE GREAT CHANGE

Author: White Deer of Autumn

$14.95 hardcover, $29.95 signed Author's Edition with two greeting-card prints from the book

Nine-year-old Wanba asks, "Why does anything have to die? Why did Grandpa have to die?" Grandma explains that just as a caterpillar "dies" only to become a beautiful butterfly, there is no death in the Circle of Life, only the Great Change. This is a story of passing on tradition, culture, and wisdom to the next generation. Watercolor illustrations throughout by internationally acclaimed painter Carol Grigg.

NOBLE RED MAN: Lakota Wisdomkeeper Mathew King

Compiler and editor: Harvey Arden, $16.95 hardcover

Lakota chief and spiritual leader Noble Red Man (Mathew King) spoke with a voice so powerful that not even death could silence him. He left behind a legacy of wisdom for us to experience and ponder in this narrative compiled by the co-author of *Wisdomkeepers*. With inspiration and insight, Noble Red Man gives voice to the struggle of Native Americans and celebrates the endurance of their spirit. An heir to the traditions left by both Crazy Horse and Sitting Bull, he applies the wisdom of the Elders to everyday personal and political situations. A tribute to honor a revered chief, this book is for those interested in history as the starting place to create the future.

WISDOMKEEPERS: Meetings with Native American Spiritual Elders
Authors: Harvey Arden and Steve Wall
Photographer: Steve Wall, $39.95 hardcover, $22.95 softcover

An extraordinary spirit-journey into the lives, minds, and natural-world philosophy of seventeen Native American spiritual Elders. They are the Old Ones, the fragile repositories of sacred ways and natural wisdom going back millennia. In the magnificent photographs and powerful words of the Wisdomkeepers, you share their innermost thoughts and feelings, their dreams and visions, their jokes and laughter, their healing remedies, and their apocalyptic prophecies. Above all, you share their humanity.

HINDSIGHTS:
The Wisdom and Breakthroughs of Remarkable People
Author: Guy Kawasaki, $22.95 hardcover

What have you learned from your life that you would like to share with the next generation? Get a fresh appreciation of the human experience in this inspirational collection of interviews with thirty-three people who have overcome unique challenges. They are candid about their failures and disappointments, and insightful about turning adversity into opportunity. Guy Kawasaki spent over two years researching and interviewing such people as Apple Computer co-founder Steve Wozniak, management guru Tom Peters, and entrepreneur Mary Kay. But not everyone in the book is a celebrity. They share their revelations and life experiences, motivating the reader for both personal and professional growth.

THE WOMAN'S BOOK OF CREATIVITY
Author: C Diane Ealy, Ph.D., $12.95 softcover, $16.95 two-tape audio set

Women are most creative when they tap into the process that is unique to their own nature—a holistic, "spiral" approach. This book is a self-help manual, both inspirational and practical, for igniting female creative fire and encouraging women to acknowledge their own creativity, often in achievements they take for granted. Ealy offers a wealth of suggestions and exercises to enable women to recognize their own creative power and to access it consistently and effectively.

SEEING WITHOUT GLASSES: Improving Your Eyesight Naturally
Author: Dr. Robert Kaplan, $12.95 softcover, $39.95 four-tape audio set

Six out of ten people depend on glasses or contacts to correct their vision. Even if you don't, you are probably experiencing some degree of eyestrain, which can result in itching, burning, and headaches. The premise of the book is stunningly simple: Eye fitness can be developed in the same way other body parts are toned—through exercise and diet. This doesn't mean throwing away your glasses or contacts, but rather learning how to use them as therapeutic tools, just as you might use a set of free weights or a racket.

LETTERS FROM THE LIGHT:
An Afterlife Journal from the Self-Lighted World
Author: Elsa Barker; Editor: Kathy Hart, $18.95 hardcover

In the early 1900s, Elsa Barker began "automatic writing." It was as if an outside force took over her hand. Later she discovered that the "author" was a judge who had died thousands of miles away, and she was serving as his conduit to tell about life after death. His descriptions of the other side convey this message: There is nothing to fear in death. Life after this one is similar in many ways to the one we already know.

THE BOOK OF GODDESSES
Author/illustrator: Kris Waldherr; Introduction: Linda Schierse Leonard, $17.95 hardcover

This beautifully illustrated book introduces readers of all ages to twenty-six goddesses and heroines from cultures around the world. In the descriptions of these archetypal women, the author weaves a picture of the beauty, individuality, and unique strength which are the birthright of every girl and woman. Beautiful to look at and inspiring to read, this book is a stunning gift for goddess-lovers of all ages.

To order or to request a catalog, contact:
Beyond Words Publishing, Inc.
4443 NE Airport Road
Hillsboro, OR 97124-6074
503-693-8700 or 1-800-284-9673